Ruby's Tale

FOR ADDY!

ENJOY THE JOURNEY....

RUBY'S TALE

A TRUE
RAGS TO RICHES
STORY

Patrick Bettendorf

Tasora

ISBN: 978-1-934690-66-6

Printed in the United States of America
Fifth Printing: 2013
14   13   12   11   5   4   3   2

Cover photograph by Kelly Whiteman, Endless Acres Photography.
    (www.endlessacresphotography.com)
Miami hospital photos by Ginger Monteleone.
Cheaper by the Dozen photo courtesy of Press Publications.
Image of Ruby kissing Bonnie Hunt courtesy of Bonnie Hunt.
Interior book design by Ryan Scheife, Mayfly Design (www.mayflydesign.net).
Front and back cover design by Lisa Tenjack - Rapid Press Printing, Inc.

BPH

Bayport Printing House, Inc.
102 Central Avenue, Bayport, MN 55003
(651) 439-3115 • www.bayportprinting.com

Tasora

Tasora Books
5120 Cedar Lake Road S
Minneapolis, MN 55416
(952) 345-4488
Distributed by Itasca Books

Contact Ruby: Rubystales@aol.com or visit www.rubystales.com

CONTENTS

ACKNOWLEDGMENTS

In putting pen to paper at the start of this book, I was reminded of that old Chinese proverb, "A journey of a thousand miles begins with a single step." I was equally mindful of the many friends, relatives, and family members whose strong vocal encouragement kept ringing in my ears: "You've got to tell Ruby's incredible story of hope!" In the telling of her tale, I stand in awe of the lives she's touched, the hearts she's opened, and the friends she has made across America. So many people, places, dogs, institutions, events, and more make up the life that is Ruby's, that I really don't know where to start or end our thanks. It's like trying keep track of every flake swirling in a snow globe. But I do know that Ruby's wonderful odyssey might not have made it into print if not for the following...

- Ron and Susie Moser, because they cared enough

- Jack Rhodes, my best friend, for pushing me on

- Total Recall School for Dogs, for its unending support

- Kathy Lahlum, for her gift of time and talent to help keep our "tribe" well trained

- All of Ruby's classmates and the rescue groups around America who voted for her

- Karen Delise, for her faith, friendship, and strong encouragement

- Stillwater Animal Hospital, for its kind, compassionate, and excellent care

- Ruby's "angel" from New York, who took care of her medical expenses when we couldn't

- Lisa Meuwissen, for her faith, encouragement, and help in getting me on that airplane

- Ryan Scheife, Ruby's book designer. He understood her story and the book shows it!

- Animal Farm Foundation

A special thanks to...

- Hotel Palomer LA Westwood

- Hard Rock Hotel–Chicago

- Kendal Hotel & Suites–Miami

- Delta Airlines

- Paul & Joan Pairitz

- Jess Andersen

- Kim Corbert

- Cheri Cunningham

- Puppy Love Caring Canines

- Ginger Monteleone

- "The Gang" at Rapid Press, Forest lake

- April Michelle Davis, my editor at Editorial Inspirations

- Ruby's legal dream team, Snyder, Gislason, Frasier LLC

**And, of course, Ruby's friends in the media who believed
in the little dog who could.**

- Rob Olson — FOX 9 News, Minneapolis/St. Paul

- Liz Collin — WCCO TV News

- Kyle Porter — KARE 11 News

- Kathy Berdan — *St. Paul Pioneer Press*

- Pat Phiffer — *Minneapolis Star Tribune*

- Kris Janisch — *Stillwater Gazette*

- Cliff Buchan — *Forest Lake Times*

- Press Publications

To my wife Lynn, who believed—even when I didn't

For Katie
1994–2004

To shelter dogs of every breed, who wait to share their hearts with a family in a forever home—may your dreams soon come true…

To pet parents of rescue dogs, for your act of love and kindness

CHAPTER ONE

It Was Only Supposed to Be for the Weekend!

Like a happy little flea, she sprang up onto the couch and flew off repeatedly. Then she tore around the little reception room like a dog gone mad, spinning as she ran. Her face smiled all the while. It was walk time! Yippie! It was October 2003, and Lynn and I were volunteers for St. Francis Animal Rescue. Because the animal rescue didn't have its own facility, it farmed out the dogs to various boarding kennels, paying discounted rates for their keep. This kennel was close to home, making it easy for us to visit twice a week.

We were known as the Rottweiler and pit bull couple. We had fostered our share and adopted many over the years. So Rotties and pitties were assigned to us. We had walked plenty of both breeds, but this happy six-month-old dark brindle pit bull mix puppy named Ruby caught our eye. There was just something extra special about her infectious, boundless, happy demeanor!

Dogs can be emotionally complex little beings. Science is only beginning to understand that fact, but anyone who has a dog as a true family member already knows this. Rescue dogs are very special cases. Many times, like foster children, they may have issues. But, most often, a pet foster parent may not know anything about the history of the animal unless abuse is obvious. Some rescue dogs may be totally resilient and optimistic. Others, no matter how much care, kindness, love, and structure they receive, have difficulty coming out of that emotional black hole. Some never do.

Ruby was an optimist. She showed no outward signs of mental or physical abuse other than starvation. Just a month or two before, Ruby and her brother had been rescued from an abandoned house, left like unwanted trash. Food and water were gone. Her fur had been falling out in patches. Lynn and I had no intention of adopting or fostering the little tyke. Yes, she was lovable, but we had enough adoptees at home. We had to tell Ruby, "Walk's over, goodbye Ruby, see you next time." If some spirit had descended upon me deep one night saying, "You and the little dog Ruby will share many adventures together, great and small. You will fly side-by-side on an airplane to distant cities and appear on national television. Her picture will be on the front of Milk-Bone boxes across the land. Ruby will receive awards and accolades. The media will print and broadcast many stories about her life and work. People in other lands will be able to read about her. Ruby will become a certified therapy dog, then someday your personal service dog. All of these things will come to pass in due time," I would have replied, "Give me a break, and let me sleep! Go away! You'd have better luck with Scrooge!" Little did I know all this would be true. But first we'd have to be forced to bring her home.

On selected Saturday mornings, Adoption Day was held at various shopping malls or big box pet stores. Ruby was but one of our charges. She sat in a generous wire cage, cute as could be. Ruby, happy to see all of the potential pet parents, was seemingly dog selective. Every time certain pooches stared in her direction, even from a distance, she'd let out a gruff, annoying bark. She would not show aggression—just that bark, bark, bark. Oddly, this was one of the only times in her life that Ruby used her voice. Later, on radio, she would be known as the narcoleptic barkless wonder dog. To this day, she rarely barks or makes a noise. During these adoption days, I started to feel more protective of Ruby—even jealous! Many people stopped by to visit with her. Of course they thought Ruby was cute, funny, and cheerful. The longer they stayed, laughing, playing, smiling, the more fear rose in me. These interlopers might actually take her home! But my job was to help her find a forever home. Seizing the opportunity, I would launch into a short educational course on the history, facts, and fiction of the breed.

"But, a pit bull? Our parents, friends, neighbors would never understand. Besides, I heard they always turn on you!" This was usually followed by a laundry list of urban legends. Were they not listening to a thing I had just said? Hold on a minute! They were no longer interested in Ruby. Whew!

Then there were those with a different agenda. "What's the biting power of these dogs?" or "When that dog is grown, could it take on a Rottweiler and beat it?"

I always replied, "Gee, I'm sorry, but we've got a hold on her until a home study is completed on a potential adopter. Please leave your name." Yet, there were a lot of great future owners who sauntered by just to chat. Luckily for me, the timing wasn't quite right for a number of reasons to add Ruby to their families. Lynn didn't know how deeply I was feeling for the jolly little dog. I dared not tell her.

Just a few days before Thanksgiving, Lynn and I were preparing to have the holiday at our house, a small, one-and-a-half story, white clapboard house built by Swedish immigrants in 1910. Except for mechanicals (wiring, heating system, windows), it still appears inside and out pretty much as it did when new. Though the house is just a thousand square feet, the traffic flow is great, which is why it works with the number of dogs sharing our lives. Still, there were a lot of guests coming on Thursday—friends, relatives, and even a couple of passersby who had nowhere to go. The place would be bursting at the seams.

The phone rang. It was the animal rescue people telling us the boarding kennel where Ruby stayed was booked for the upcoming holiday weekend with regular-paying customers. The rescue dogs had to be put up elsewhere. Could we take Ruby just for the holiday?

Lynn was firm. No! Sorry, but we're slammed, too.

It was the first of three calls over two days. By the last one, they were desperate. "There's just no room at the inn!"

Lynn's resistance had been worn down. She reluctantly agreed. "Just for the weekend. Monday, she goes back. We're not going to foster her!"

I naturally professed agreement. Lynn had a legitimate point. We did have enough dogs, but I secretly hoped Ruby would win Lynn over.

Thanksgiving Day arrived. The wonderful aroma of turkey, freshly baked rolls, and pies wafted through the air. This was not lost on Katie, Carla, Hilde, Venus, and Tiger, as we banished them, disgruntled, to the upstairs bedrooms. Ruby had her own crate on the enclosed front porch with a view of the entire dining area. After dinner when most of the guests were feeling lethargic, Lynn suggested I let Ruby out of her cage.

"Let's see how she does."

Slipping out of the crate, Ruby did a little skip-run that seemed to be uniquely her style. Instead of blasting to where the action was, she skipped from room to room, giving everyone a quick once over. "Hi, I'm Ruby! Oh you smell good. I'll be back. Hey, you look like fun."

After the initial greeting, she went back to each person to get better acquainted. She was showing manners—impeccable manners, in fact. She did not leap on and off the furniture like a gazelle. She did not try to snatch food from the table. Ruby hopped up between two people on the couch, carefully turned to face the room, and sat quietly. She seemed to be carefully studying the room and the guests. It was as if she were formulating some kind of plan.

"If I play my paws right, I'll be running this place in six months. When I meet the pack, my being submissive and happy will win them over. Then, it's rise through the ranks, not by fierce fang and claw. But I'll outsmart, outwit, and outplay them. This behaving-well business seems to be working on the humans around here. Oops! The hosts are watching me. If I curl up on this guy's lap and pretend to sleep, it'll be really cute."

Even with all the company, Lynn and I observed Ruby's wheels turning. We thought it was a hoot.

My mother-in-law piped up. "You can't send her back! She's the perfect dog. Awww, look at the poor thing sleeping on your father's lap. How sweet!"

Holy cow! Help from an unexpected source. Outgunned, her resistance once again flagging, poor Lynn couldn't hold out much longer. She clearly was not entirely happy with the prospect of another mouth to feed, more veterinarian expenses, and increased care in general. Lynn was always the practical one about such things.

"She is awfully nice." A long pause. "Oh sure, what's one more? Five, six, not much difference."

It was a done deal! Ruby had found her forever home.

CHAPTER TWO

The Family Pack

Ruby's assimilation into the family was remarkably smooth. She loved her new pack and her new home! The house was small, but the yard was big. With almost an acre enclosed with a chain-link fence, it was a great place to run, jump, play, and tear it up!

Ruby was soon attending obedience classes at Total Recall School for Dogs, one of the most respected training schools in the Midwest, run by retired K-9 Cop Glenn Kothe and his wife and excellent trainer, Sue. The school had "special rates" for rescue dogs. Ruby's first few sessions were challenging. It was like trying to train a cat. She seemed to say, "I don't mind being cute, hanging around the house, and planning my takeover, but this? Ugh!" But something clicked by about the fourth week, and she started to fast-forward, excelling in the class. A number of training centers didn't allow some breeds, like pit bulls, based on their reputation. But out of the thousands of dogs that went through the system, Total Recall had never had a problem with so-called dangerous breeds. Not one bite had ever occurred.

Other family pack members liked Ruby, finding no threat in her presence. The cagey little dog continued to take mental notes...the other dogs' behaviors, car-riding etiquette, and daily routines. She was a fast learner, soon settling into an easy rhythm. I would be remiss if I didn't share something about the canine characters Ruby lived with—those she played with, roughhoused with, sometimes scuffled and traveled with, and learned from, each with their own distinct personality.

Katie (Rottweiler, 1994–2004)

Katie was the canine pack leader. At nine, she was the oldest member when Ruby joined the pack. Katie ruled with a velvet paw. She was never physically challenged for her position. She often took her lead from me to keep things under control. For instance, to break it up if the others were playing too rough, she simply would blast between the offenders, knocking them over like bowling pins. (Ruby learned the technique well, using it to full effect later on.)

Years before, I had a sixty-five-pound, seventeen-year-old mixed breed that had developed doggie dementia in the last six months of his life, wandering off my property before it was fenced in. This was something he had never done before. I would say, "Katie, bring back Champ." We went to round him up. After showing her twice what I meant, it became her job. She never let him out of the yard again, gently nudging him around toward the house whenever he tried to leave.

I liked to startle guests with, "Katie! Bring them a coaster please," or, "Please throw this in the trash." It was fun to watch their faces when she did! Katie was exceptionally smart and wise and a certified therapy dog.

We had many wonderful adventures of our own. There was a profound inner connection I'm sure I will never have again, but I feel blessed for having experienced it. Ruby taught me I could have something special with another dog. I love all our dogs, but it's just not the same as that "one."

When Katie passed away, the pack was thrown into a tailspin. I might have been the ultimate alpha, but it was clear that Katie did my bidding in terms of monitoring pack behavior and keeping things on an even keel. No one ascended to take her place. They were either too immature, didn't want the job, or simply were not sharp enough. Ruby learned a lot from Katie in the short time they had together and developed many of her qualities. It would have been interesting if Ruby had had a year or two more with Katie.

Carla (Rottweiler, 2001 –   )

A smallish example of the breed, Carla is the class clown. Sensitive, smart, pretty, cute, and fun, Carla was the youngest household member until Ruby arrived. A momma's girl, she would lay at Lynn's feet all day as Lynn telecommuted in her front porch office. Life was good for Carla.

She had not a care in the world until her best friend, Hannah, died not long after Ruby's arrival. Just recovering from that loss, Carla was then struck with Katie passing away eight months later. BOOM! She spiraled down a dark tunnel to a place that was sad and terrible and frightening. She became withdrawn, skittish, fearful of everything, and snappish with strangers. She even nipped a cop on the hand when he reached down to pet her. Lucky for us all, he was a fan of the breed, understanding her sad tale.

Carla's eating was spotty. The happy brightness had left her eyes. She was truly like a ship without a rudder. Carla mentally left us for more than two years, living among us like a ghost. It was so heartbreaking and the damndest thing I had ever seen.

But Carla battled back, enduring some serious health issues along the way. At eight years of age, she began acting like the young, happy dog she used to be. The light returned in her eyes and was beautiful to see.

Another delight to see was Carla taking on the responsibility of nanny to the little girl we adopted. It was a job she relished with great care and tenderness. If Carla has a fault, it is that she watches too much television and doesn't much care for dogs on the screen. They don't even have to be barking. Another thing she hates is people who sneak up on something. This is met with a low, nasty growl. Watching her watch television is more entertaining than anything on the tube. Carla is now an older dog, and we know time is not on our side, so we live each day grateful to have her back.

Tiger (Rescue Pit Bull, 1998–)

We met the dog that would change our minds about pit bulls at an adoption day function years before Ruby came along. "Mr. T" was five years old and sharing a pen with a young black Lab. Tiger was wrestling, with his tail wagging and mouth agape in a big happy smile. With a beautiful light tan brindle coat, Tiger was low to the ground and broad across the beam. His ears were nonexistent, cropped tight to his skull, and he had a strange, unsteady gate—a kind of weird side-to-side waffling motion, frightening really. But his eyes were soft and kind with traces of sadness. I liked him! After I petted and played with Tiger for awhile, the volunteers told me that he needed a foster home. I hunted Lynn down in another part of the store. "Honey, I want to show you something. Ta da! Isn't he pretty?"

Lynn clearly wasn't as impressed. "Well, sort of. Scary looking, too!"

Uh-oh, I hadn't planned on her noticing that part. "He's really sweet. Can we foster him?" As most guys in a situation like this, I behaved like an excited young boy.

Reality quickly followed. "Patrick, are you out of your mind?! A pit bull?!"

I pleaded, "It's only to foster!"

Unmoved, Lynn uttered, "Unh-unh…no way!"

I slunked away, defeated, to pout for awhile.

Starting that night, I read everything I could about the breed. A lot of it certainly wasn't flattering. A lot of digging was required to disseminate fact from fiction from urban legends.

A couple of weeks later, we were at yet another adoption day event. There was Tiger in the first pen for all to see! "Hey look, Lynn, there's my buddy."

This time, she lingered, her eyes washing over Tiger again and again, surveying every movement. Finally, "Well, he does seem like a good boy. Gets along with other dogs."

Not wanting to bring up that *foster* word again, I casually asked, "What do you think?"

"Well, okay, we can give it a try."

Wow! That was too easy! Tiger was able to come with us immediately—the animal rescue group was familiar with Lynn and me because of our experience with Rottweilers. We signed a few papers and were off to meet some friends at a dog show in downtown St. Paul. In our hurry, we did two really dumb things that would definitely fall into the "What were we thinking?" category.

Katie was waiting in the car out in the parking lot. I held Tiger on a leash while Lynn hooked up Katie. In the middle of the lot, they had a quick meet and greet. The two got along like fast friends. Katie jumped into the car first, and then Tiger followed. She was a perfect host. He respected her. This, however, was not a good idea, and things could have gone very badly. Once we arrived at the dog show, we at least had the presence of mind to know that the two shouldn't be left alone together.

"We can't leave Tiger alone in the car," Lynn said. "We don't know if he'll chew up the seats." So it was Tiger who would come inside with us, but how to get him in? Quickly, a half-baked plan was hatched. We took turns without Tiger entering the building, buying a ticket, going to another entrance, getting stamped, meeting back at the car, grabbing Tiger, and re-entering via the exhibitors' entrance that was manned by an unsuspecting teenager. Oh, we felt like criminals.

Once inside, the challenges changed. People were frightened by Tiger's appearance with that wafflely gate and the hack job on his ears. Then they would turn their attention to us with an expression that clearly said, "How could you do that?!" Yet, there was puzzlement. We didn't act or dress like the pit bull owners depicted by the media.

A couple of judges picked up our scent and followed us. Finally they closed in. "Excuse me," the beefier, middle-aged judge panted out as if he had run a marathon. "That dog doesn't belong here. How did you get in?!"

I said, "Oh, I'm sorry. Aren't we allowed to bring the dogs into this area?"

He asked, "Where did you come from?" Taken aback by my instant answer and sugary sweet concern, he was confused.

I responded, "We're doing doggie demos over in the retail arena."

Seemingly more confused he retorted, "What?"

I had him on the run as I smoothly answered, "Agility demos. To share with people the fun they can have with their dog. Today we're using rescue dogs."

"Oh," they both seemed satisfied.

I made one final stab at bravado. "It's break time now, but stop by later and we'll show you what agility is all about."

The older one spoke this time, "We *know* what agility is!" They moved on. I thought to myself, *Dear God, I'm going to hell. No trial. Nothing.* Lynn and I made a hasty retreat to the real agility ring where we sat up high and out of sight in the balcony. Our friends did find us that day, but were left wondering why we enjoyed sitting up so high. It's embarrassing to think about this little adventure today, and it bothers me to think that there are a couple of guys out there who have my image in their mind's eye as a rogue and a liar.

As usual in rescue dogs, we knew nothing about Tiger's past, but in the coming months and years we caught glimpses. Motorcycles. He loved motorcycles. Anything that sounded like a Harley-Davidson woke something deep within him. If we were out for a walk and a Harley started up with that signature blast, Tiger would pull up short, with tail wagging and head bobbing, to see if there was anyone he knew from his past. When the motorcycle roared off, he would watch until it disappeared. It was a sad sight to see.

We called him "the locksmith." Gate latches, doorknobs, double-hung window locks, and sliding window latches were all of great interest to Tiger. He would poke and prod, even try using a tooth to manipulate them. This was just one of the unsolved mysteries of Tiger.

Tiger was thin coated and hated the cold. If the house was the least bit chilly, we would find him curled up tightly, shivering. The first time we saw that, Lynn said, "Poor guy, let's put a blanket over him." When I attempted to cover him, Tiger rocketed out of the room, running to the back porch and hiding under the table, not budging for two days. We couldn't tempt him with food, water, or meaty treats. What terrible thing happened to the poor guy?! It was a couple of weeks before things were more or less back to normal.

Tiger's waffling gate was the product of enormous muscle mass on a hodgepodge skeletal frame no doubt caused by bad breeding. He also had a notch in his spine caused by a blow from a pipe or board, which caused untold problems. So there you have it…an abused rescue dog with issues, both physical and mental, leaving the adopter to pick up the pieces. With love, patience, and direction, the big lug led a good life after coming to live with us. We are proud to know him and grateful that he allowed us to live with him and be part of his life.

Tiger lived up to his namesake, very cat-like and independent. Always a gentleman, if one of the girls finished her food before him and approached his bowl looking for more, Tiger always stepped aside to let her chow down. Always. So, we sat beside him at breakfast and dinner, guarding his meal from those canine sirens. In his old age, his bones started to betray him, making his strange gait even more pronounced. Slower and tiring more easily, he was nonetheless content and happy. And on chilly nights when we covered him up with his blanket, Tiger gave us that little snorting noise Lynn and I came to know so well. It was an approving "Thank you, everything is okay."

Hilde (Rottweiler, 1995–2008)

I purchased Hilde from a breeder who ignored her as opposed to abusing her. I felt badly for the young dog. At six months old, she had both rear legs broken, the bones snapped off by the heel. I never did buy the explanation of how it happened: "A jump and turn in the short dog run and they just popped." I always suspected the breeder's boyfriend. He was a nasty, very vindictive, and disagreeable man. The kennel owner, a widow we'll call Ms. Delany, had two homes out in the country with connecting property lines. The boyfriend asked Ms. Delany to temporarily sign over one of the properties to him because he had to have more equity to secure a loan he needed for his business. Unbelievably, she agreed! Shortly after the papers were filed, he dumped her! Ms. Delany took him to court, but the smooth talker was able to convince the judge it was a gift. During the ensuing months, her now ex-boyfriend harassed her in every possible way.

When I brought Hilde into the drama-free peace and quiet of

my home, her legs were supposedly healed. This was not so. Both quickly snapped again. At the vet, X-rays showed no repair work had previously been done. I contacted one of the best orthopedic surgeons in the Twin Cities. It would be $2,500 to repair both legs, but the doctor warned me that he'd seen a number of Rotties with honeycomb bones. If that were her case, then the prognosis would be poor. The doctor said that putting Hilde to sleep would be the most humane thing to do.

I had to think about my options for a few days. My theater company was doing pretty well, and I had a fair salary (by nonprofit standards). But I was single and had a house to pay for, and I was bringing the mechanicals up-to-date on the wonderful old place. A solution sat in my garage. I decided to sell my collector car, a 1965 Ford Falcon Coupe that I had just finished restoring. It now looked like it had just rolled off the delivery truck. Lightweight with a "built" 289, it was fast and fun but had to go. It sold quickly, and I never looked back.

Hilde was to get the chance she deserved! I hung around in the veterinarian's waiting room to find out if her bones could take the pins and wires needed. During surgery, a tech came out to tell me it was a go! What a happy moment! What a relief! Teary eyed, I left for breakfast to celebrate.

It was a long recovery process with Hilde spending much time in her crate and on a leash, even for her potty breaks. In time, she healed beautifully. The doctor thought her legs might bother her in old age, but they never did give her any real difficulties. Only in brutally cold weather did they give her some trouble. After just a few minutes outside, Hilde would raise her back-end off the ground, walking like a circus dog on her front feet. Back inside, she'd warm up and be on all four feet in a couple of moments. I suspected it was the metal pins used in repairing her damaged legs.

She was a very pretty Rott with lots of color (meaning lots of tan) on her face. She was a good, very obedient, and seemingly grateful dog her whole life, though somewhat frantic in nature—a 90-pound Chicken Little.

At times, it could be amusing, other times not so much. To the very end of her life, she liked nothing better than cuddling, being close, and touching. When she was thirteen and it was time to say the final good-bye, Hilde closed her eyes in dreamy pleasure as I stroked her soft fur and velvety ears, telling her she was a good girl. Then she was gone.

I had never dropped off a furry family member at the veterinarian's office whose time had come. They had gone many paths in life with me, good and bad. They had always stayed true and loving, never cheating, never lying, and always happy to see me. They had comforted me in the darkest times and shared my unbridled joy. They had never broken my heart…until this day. It was the least I could do, to be at the crossroads of the path they must now take alone. To say good-bye and thank-you for sharing their lives with me, to say I'll see you on the other side. I love you.

Venus (Rescue Rottweiler, 2001–)

If Venus could talk, she would have sounded exactly like the Disney character Goofy. She was a sweet dog and was always jumpity-jump happy to see us for walk time. But she was also possibly the dumbest Rottie I had ever known. A constant dopey expression rode her innocent face—a kind of "Gee, what's goin' on? Yup, yup" look. She was a dog on the walk list whenever we arrived at the kennel to work with the rescue dogs boarded there. Given her very large frame, the poor dog was underweight by about forty pounds.

Judging by her teats, Venus had recently had puppies, but they were not with her when she was found wandering. For a very long time afterward, Venus would let loose a pitiful whimpering cry when she saw puppies, attempting to get closer to them. And, she had been shot. A small caliber bullet was lodged near her right hip. The doctor said it wasn't causing a problem. "Just leave it alone."

Her coat wasn't a nice, rich dark black, but a dull, dry grayish black. She had a bad case of dandruff. Certainly, life on the lam didn't agree with Venus. Despite it all, she was loving and affectionate. At times, she was way over the top. It was as if she were trying to say, "Oh please please please love me!" We'd be completely smothered. She would have made a great dog for a single-dog family. But nobody wanted her.

She had been adopted a couple of times but brought back as "unsuitable," "didn't fit in," and "caused a problem." But in fact, as is many times the case, the adopters didn't give her a chance, didn't do their homework, or were just plain foolish.

One of them even admitted, "Gee, I bought a nice cage and everything. We wanted Venus to get to know our neighbors and family so we had a party. Everybody came to our house, even the dogs. She was sitting in her cage in the living room. When my dad went up to say 'hi,' she gave him a horrible growl! Everyone was scared. Dad said to take her back." The poor dog hadn't been in the people's house twenty-four hours when this "incident" occurred. Lynn and I received the call from animal rescue about 8:30 p.m. to meet the adopters at a gas station and take Venus back. They couldn't wait until the next day. It had to be that night. Another couple wanted her strictly as a guard dog, but that was not about to happen! She came to stay with us in her new forever home.

Venus did have some hidden talents and a strange lack of abilities. She could catch better than just about any dog I knew. She made it look easy and casual—food, balls, paper cups, sticks, bones,

Lynn's underwear; it didn't matter. Let me offer an explanation on that last item.

Venus visited me from time to time while I was doing laundry downstairs. I'd toss her the closest thing at hand to catch. Unfortunately, most times it happened to be Lynn's frilly underthings. When I attempted to recover the item, Venus, thinking it great sport, started playing tug-o-war. This is something we do not encourage. It didn't take much pulling, and they were, well, frilly after all, and ripped in one fashion or another. At first I thought this funny, especially when Lynn mentioned that some of her underwear had been wrecked in the laundry. She asked that I check the machine for sharp edges, as she couldn't find any. When a few more pairs were damaged, I happened upon Lynn making a call to Sears, bitterly complaining about the rotten washing machine ruining her best undergarments. Not so funny anymore, I had to fess up. With a lot of hems and haws, I finally proffered up my admission of guilt. Lynn was not amused. I had not thought of the underwear tossing as sick entertainment. To me, it was just finding common ground with a dog who had not had much fun in her previous life. My lame excuse did not hold much water with Lynn. I was asked to call Sears and confess that it was my odd behavior that was the problem with destroying her underwear, not the great washing machine.

Venus loved cats and always wanted to be near them. If she were lucky enough to run into a dog-tolerant cat, she would clean them like a newborn puppy. This is something cats do not enjoy.

Venus was an inventive player with toys, especially large balls. Basketballs were terrific, but jolly balls (big, thick rubber balls with handles) were the absolute tops! She'd roll them to and up the fence. Then, with a flip of the nose, the ball would fly up and backward over her head bouncing off her back. Then it became a fierce enemy shaken to death. Hmmm, pretty smart for such a dumb dog.

Venus always loved being part of the family, but the one thing she never could grasp was how to play with the other dogs. Lord knows she wanted to, but her idea of play was a constant hard porpoising to the ribs, gaining nothing but the other's great displeasure. Or, worse yet, she would try to ride them. A serious violation in their eyes! I suspect it was an attempt at rising to the alpha position. After a few times of trying that stunt, I swear the other dogs fell down and rolled onto their backs laughing. If they banned her from playing, poor Venus would stand there and continuously bark. Six years later, she still hadn't learned any of the family play nuances. But Venus did pass her Therapy Dogs International requirements to become a certified therapy dog. No doubt about it, she was a member of our pack.

Molly (Rescue Pit Bull/Black Lab, 2007–   )

Molly was the youngest member of our "tribe," as some of our family and friends affectionately called us. She was the unintended, unexpected, unprepared for, unwanted adoption. Lynn and I had never held up our work with Pitties and Rotties for all to see. We never had a public campaign to say, "Bring us your down-trodden, your poor, your hungry, your huddled shivering, flea-infested, abused dogs." People just seemed to have heard about us.

Molly was found by a couple, not far from their home in St. Paul. About six to eight months old, she was tied to a fence, her collar so tight she could hardly breathe. This couple happened to go to the same training school as Lynn and I. They didn't know us personally, but our reputation was at work. Word on the street was "Oh yes, Pat and Lynn will take any dog of those breeds [Rotties and Pitties]. They'll say no at first but just work 'em over awhile and voila—the dog is no longer your burden."

These temporary keepers of Molly called us after sneakily

19

obtaining our unlisted phone number. They pleaded her case...how they had found her...what a nice but somewhat timid girl she was...and so very cute! They would absolutely keep her except their dogs didn't like her. Taking Molly to the shelter wasn't an option. Being a black dog, there was not much hope of adoption, and most likely she would be put down. "We know you have class tonight. Could you just take a peek at her?"

This time, both Lynn and I dug in our heels. Yes, we would take a peek, no we would not take the dog home! Arriving at the school a little early, we met the dog we said no to. They were right: She was cute. Molly was all black with a nice, white blaze from under the chin spilling down her chest with feet that seemed too big. Pit bull feet are compact and look like bulldog feet, which also look like boxer feet. These were large, webbed black Lab feet. I thought out loud. "She ought to do well in snow. Sort of a doggie version of a snowshoe hare!"

The comment was met with faint smiles and half-hearted nods. Ignoring my poke at humor, the "Molly keepers" moved in for the coupe de grace and opened up a rapid-fire barrage. "She has her first set of shots. We've got a big bag of high-quality dog food and a really nice new toy. She's very smart. We can't keep her. Nobody wants her. We don't want her to die."

Whew! The attack left me swaying like a punch-drunk pugilist. I looked up at Lynn. She walked away stiff legged, knowing what was about to happen.

Then the couple, like car salesmen sensing a deal was at hand, threw something else into the pot that they hoped would be the clincher. "We'll for sure help find her a permanent home. Molly just can't stay with us. Right now she's living in the dark, unheated garage, and it's getting cold!"

That did it! I thought of our family snug in our beds at night.

Now if I said no, Molly's shivering little face would appear in front of me every night, every day, every time I...Oh hell! All the time! All right. Okay, you can stop now. I'll take the dog!

"Great! Your dogs don't know Molly, so after class we'll follow you home. Oh! By the way, she gets car sick." It was a long ride home with Lynn. The only words spoken eluded to my mental condition, the fact that she was going to China next month to pick up our adoptive daughter, Sadie, and we did not need this, this thing! Then followed the dreaded silence. I deserved her prolonged significant anger. I admit—I was a sap, a sucker, a sentimental fool, prone to do such inconsiderate things. When Lynn left for China, I tried to make up for my indiscretion by deep-cleaning and reorganizing the house. The result was that Lynn could not find things in a nice, clean house when she returned. She did appreciate my efforts, though.

In the meantime, Dr. Rice, our veterinarian who was familiar with our mom-and-pop rescue efforts, donated his services to spay Molly. Getting her rescue dog discount, she started her beginner obedience classes at Total Recall. Because we already had Carla and Ruby in intermediate training, Molly was handled by Kathy, a good friend with a lot of experience. Molly was smart, learning everything quickly. She excelled at heeling and recalls. Her downfalls were jumping happily up on people or a loud, annoying whining when there was a lull in the class. These were two items that needed extra attention. And then a disaster demonstrated that we needed to redouble our efforts to curb that jumping. Kathy came to class dressed for comfort in a nice comfy sweatshirt and sweatpants. Comfort was always a good idea. One evening at a most inopportune moment during class, Molly jumped on Kathy as if to say, "Hey! Am I doing okay?" Her paws caught inside the pants pockets. Kathy commanded, "OFF!" Molly retreated downward, taking the pants partially down with her.

21

Since Molly joined our family, she has been a wonderful ambassador for pit bull mixes. Though slow to mature, with a higher energy level than the others, Molly turned out to be a good, obedient dog, blending smoothly into the family unit. Molly loved to roughhouse with Tiger. He would return the favor to the best of his ability given his advanced age. When Ruby felt it was too much horseplay, she put an end to it, pronto. Ultimately, Molly respected and was drawn to Ruby. They were very close, sleeping together a lot. They fit together like pieces of a puzzle. Molly can learn much from Ruby. The torch will be passed on some day, and I hope that Molly will have the maturity to handle it with the same class and dignity as Ruby.

As for the couple who was going to help us find a home for Molly, neither hide nor hair has been seen of them. They even quit the obedience school.

So there you have it—our family pack. Not the life for everyone, but it is certainly a rewarding one for us. As I think about our family, I am reminded of that starfish story by Loren Eiseley:

A wise man walking along the beach happened upon a young man throwing objects into the ocean. "May I ask what it is you are doing?"

The young man paused, looked up, and replied, "I am throwing starfish into the ocean."

"I must ask, why are you throwing them into the ocean?" asked the wise man.

To this, the young man replied, "The sun is up and the tide is going out. If I don't throw them in, they'll die."

Hearing this, the wise man commented, "But young man, there are miles and miles of beaches with starfish all along the way. You can't possibly make a difference!"

At this, the young man bent down and picked up yet another starfish and threw it into the ocean. "I made a difference to that one."

And so it is with us. We're just trying to make a difference, one unwanted dog at a time.

CHAPTER THREE

What Makes Me...Me!

Over the years, I was asked many times, "What's this thing you have about dogs? Is it a power trip? Why would anyone have so many when there are lots of children in the world who need help?" Those questions made me bristle.

If you picked up this book, most likely you are a dog person and know the answer to those questions. It was not about power over another living being or that we hated kids. There was just something deep inside us driving us to protect and speak up for these lovely creatures who have no voice. There are a goodly number of well-written scientific books on the truly incredible human–canine relationship.

That is not the focus here. It is about Ruby, the people, the dogs, the decisions, the twists and turns and happenstance that brought us together, propelling her and our family on a wonderful, sometimes wild ride. We all carry forward some sort of baggage, trauma, and tough times, whatever you want to call it. It seems to me that how we handle it molds our future behavior. Here, then, is just a sliver of events in my early life that set in motion a long pattern of behavior, which helped my life to cross paths with Ruby's.

Three things haunted me. The first two may well account in large measure for my relationship with dogs. As a boy in second grade, I was very close with my oldest brother, Skip, who bought, with his own money, a black Lab puppy shortly before his seventeenth birthday. Buddy (named after Buddy Holly) was the apple of my eye. Rushing home from school to play with the chubby, tail-wagging pup was the highlight of every day. Skip, always patient with my trying to monopolize Buddy's time, had planned to train him for duck hunting. But on a pretty spring day as I walked home from school, Brian, my second-oldest brother, out of breath from running around trying to find me, said Skip had been killed in an accident. He had been on his motorcycle with a friend in a car behind him. Supposedly, the friend tried to scare Skip, misjudged the distance, and hit him from behind. Through the shock and sorrow of losing Skip, I clung tightly to Buddy. His fur soaked up plenty of tears.

There was no relationship between the surviving siblings and myself. They were teenagers with other things to do besides wipe my nose. So Buddy, like Skip, was my friend. But Buddy still waited for Skip to come home every day, sitting by his doghouse, watching the driveway. It was a difficult sight to watch.

One day, returning home from school, I saw that Buddy wasn't there. There was no tail wagging, no happy face to greet me. Mom couldn't stand to see the dog waiting for my brother and told my dad to get rid of it. The story I was told was that Buddy went to a "good home." It was shattering. But like most kids, I eventually moved on, having good friends nearby to keep me busy, but Buddy never left my heart.

It was a year or two later when Dad brought home a German shepherd/husky mix. An adult dog, it had been tied outside while neighborhood kids threw snowballs, rocks, or anything they could grab and toss at the poor thing. It was not a good idea to bring a dog that had suffered such abuse into our home. No one had the experience or know-how to handle such a beast. He was large, about a hundred pounds. He was food aggressive and aggressive with children and with the family.

But, by God, Dad got him for free! Husky was a tormentor of my sister. If she came home late, Husky ripped and shred her clothes. It's been rumored that my sister's shrill screams are still hanging out over East St. Paul somewhere. To the best of my memory, he never did bite her, but a number of her best things were left in tatters. Whenever we left the house, upon our return he wouldn't let us in. After a couple of terrifying rounds of that, my dad locked Husky in the basement before we left.

When we arrived back home, Dad would try to let him out a little at a time, but it was to no avail. Husky blasted the door open, pushing anyone nearby off to the side. We prayed he'd recognize us before he killed us. Oddly, the dog liked me well enough, but was not loving or cuddly like Buddy.

I remember thinking how mad I was at those kids for being so mean and making the dog the way he was. Soon enough Husky also went to a "good home." Years later, Dad admitted that he drove far out to the country, let him go, and drove off. I was so ashamed of him at the time. Unfortunately, that's just what people did with unwanted pets back then, and some people still do it today. I thought of Buddy sharing the same fate, but could not ask, preferring to think and hope that he went to a good forever home.

In my freshman year of high school, we moved to a small horse farm in the country while Dad commuted to his job in the Twin Cities. Having left my friends in the old neighborhood, I was ready for my very own dog. Mom had her dog, Ginger, a pit bull mix. A good dog to be sure, but make no mistake about it—she belonged to Mom, and Mom wasn't about to share her. Besides, that dog never left her sight.

In the back of my mind, I knew Mom didn't want another dog around, but we had one hundred and twenty acres, and with surrounding farms, the exploration possibilities were endless! (This was before I had discovered girls could be pretty fun, too!) The new dog I would get someday soon and I would bound through fields and forests sharing all kind of adventures. We'd stay out of Mom's way. She couldn't, wouldn't care! But I had to wait for just the right moment.

My math teacher, unfortunately, helped screw up the timing of my plan. He brought to school a chubby, female, tan-and-white collie mix puppy. "She's a stray, but my wife is having a baby and we can't keep her. I know you want a dog. Can you take her?"

She was beautiful. That puppy smell was wonderful. She liked me! "Yes! I'll take her!"

Then almost as an afterthought, he asked, "Will it be okay with your parents?"

Without thinking, I blurted out, "Sure! We have lots of room!"

The bus driver allowed the dog to ride on my lap all the way home. (Try that today.) He was curious, "What's the dog's name?"

I clearly remember saying, "Queenie." It came out of nowhere, but it stuck.

As the orange bus creaked, bounced, and rattled onto the final stretch of road before my house, a sudden and awful fear rose in my chest. My heart was beating like a rabbit. I thought it was going to explode. The excitement about the dog faded and was replaced with a "What have I done?" dread. Mom was not a woman to cross, disobey, or trifle with. She was an unpredictable person with a dark soul and a violent temper. This was not going to be good. The old brakes squealed the bus to a stop at our driveway. I trembled down the steps onto the gravel, and the safety of my steel cocoon took off in a cloud of dust.

There we were, Queenie, wearing the new collar my teacher bought her with little more than string for a leash, and me, wishing the bus would return.

It was too late. Walking up to the house from the barn, Mom spotted my new partner. "Whose dog?"

Pausing a second or two to gather my courage, I bleated out, "Her name is Queenie and she's mine." I quickly told the story of the math teacher, his wife having a baby...everything and then some, how the dog wouldn't be a bother to her or Ginger. Bracing myself for what was sure to come, I was shocked by her response.

Mom just looked at the two of us for what seemed like forever, studying us as if we were a couple of miscreants. Turning away, almost casually, she said, "The dog can't stay in the house."

There was no slapping or punching. This was good. It seemed like a tacit "Yes, you can keep the dog." I should have known by the quiet tone of her voice that trouble was brewing.

In the following days after school, Queenie and I spent every waking minute together, setting up a comfortable place for her in the barn, bounding around the countryside, making plans how and where we would live together someday.

I can't remember exactly how many days we shared, five? Seven? Nine? That part is fuzzy. But what is crystal clear is hopping off the bus one late September day. I hot-footed over to the barn where Queenie was waiting. When I threw open the door, instead of the happy whimpering that always greeted me, there was silence. Something was wrong! In a panic, I rushed to her spot. Everything was gone—the large wooden box surrounded by hay bales, her raggedy blanket, the water and food bowls, Ginger's old discarded chew toy, everything! An awful, hollow ache rose inside my chest, a terrible anguish. I ripped up to the house screaming, "Queenie is gone! What did you do with her, Mom? Mom!"

Her answer is as chilling today as it was so long ago. "I shot her! You knew I didn't want another dog around here and still you brought it home!"

I stumbled backward. I could not believe my ears. I had never shown verbal disrespect toward Mom. (I knew better.) This day would be different, and I paid the price. But the damage had been done. Queenie was gone. I guess bringing home a dog without permission was not respectful. Perhaps. But it certainly didn't warrant that kind of response. Also, why was it that she let me keep the dog for a number of days? I believe it was a control issue...letting us bond and then taking Queenie away in such a violent manner. Tough stuff. Better analyzed by an expert. Through it all, I made a promise that when I was on my own, I would take care of dogs nobody wanted. And no one could say a thing. What bothers me still is that in saying yes to bringing that chubby little puppy home, I signed her death warrant.

In 1984, Spatz, the latest in a line of rescue dogs, accompanied me on a trip to Seattle. We were planning to visit my dad's sister whose health had been failing. I loved road trips. Slow, yes, but rich in a texture of people, scenery, foods, and cultural differences. You can linger awhile in a place you like, if you have the time. Unexpected adventure may lie around the very next turn. Sometimes, you might not like what you discover. Cruising through Montana, Spatz and I decided to take a potty break and stretch our legs a bit. Pulling into a rest stop, we set about taking care of business. That done, it was time to get the "kinks" out. It was a gorgeous spot overlooking a panorama of mountains. Almost immediately, we discovered an Australian shepherd shot to death at the brush line. Dreadful memories came flooding back. What terrible thing happened? Why? Did the dog piddle in the car, the father or mother go on a rant and do this terrible act? In front of their children? Or was it something else? A million questions, but no answers. This beautiful place was now only a sad, lonely windswept hill.

CHAPTER FOUR

Ruby Goes to Work

From the first moment on that Thanksgiving Day 2003, I felt that Ruby had the temperament to be a therapy dog. I had done two years of research on pit bulls and also worked hands-on with a number of them. Plus I had eight years' experience as a pet therapy program volunteer. It was a no-brainer, and I wasn't worried one whittle. Ruby was kind, snuggly, and friendly, but not overwhelmingly so. And she had those manners...a kind of a doggie social decorum. Oh sure, the first four weeks of obedience school seemed more for her entertainment than anything else. But she was young, had a short attention span, and thought the world revolved around her...hmmm, a lot like me in my youth.

By spring 2005, I felt she was ready to take the Therapy Dogs International (TDI) test. A dog must pass all fourteen criteria, or the dog would fail. The TDI test looked for how the dog reacted to petting, brushing, wheelchairs, walkers, strange or unfamiliar movement, sudden noises, children, and other dogs. How do they walk on a leash and behave when left alone for a few minutes?

I had every confidence Ruby would pass. Everything went great until one of the last parts of the test. A person with a leashed dog on his left side walked toward Ruby, and I walked in their direction.

The idea was to meet, shake hands with the other person, make small talk for a moment, and then go on our merry way. The dogs were not to make contact with each other. Damn! Wouldn't you know that the other canine was a Rottweiler. We have Rotties at home! The sight of the large black bruiser made Ruby very happy. Forgetting herself for a moment, she quickly crossed over to say a friendly "Hi!" I started to trip and wobble. Test over.

By November 2005, we were ready to test again. Working with friends, Ruby went through the drill over and over. We had it nailed—except for that saying "Hi" to the other dog monkey business. That part was spotty. Still, we went for the test. Apparently, Ruby knew it was for real. This go 'round she passed with flying colors. Within two weeks, she was volunteering at two healthcare residences each week.

I like senior citizens. I learned some four decades ago that they are living, breathing history books. My entire life had been spent entertaining them, bringing them smiles, laughs, a little happiness and brightness to their days. It was all due to my best friend's little sister, Cathy, in 1969.

As a child, she spent a lot of time at a children's hospital due to a serious birth defect. During her long periods confined to a hospital bed, her brother and I would visit. Seeing these kids twisted and broken, in pain, broke my heart. I hated the hand dealt to Cathy and the other kids in her ward. After seeing the difficulty they had to go through each day, I just started going back to the hospital more often on my own. At first it was pure guilt. I was young, healthy, and living on my own. I drove a hot muscle car and chased girls. I had it too good. After a number of times just hanging around talking with the kids, an idea hatched in my head out of the blue.

At the time, I was dabbling in acting and had done some fairly decent impressions of popular actors, politicians, and TV personalities of the time. *Hey,* I thought, *these kids are bored, they need something else in the way of entertainment.* I put together, in retrospect, a pretty lame routine and tried it out on Cathy and the kids. They had a blast! And I felt damn good. From that afternoon to this day, I have had a direction and have felt appreciated. The nurses asked me to visit other kids. All right! This is good fun, but let's take it another step forward. Gillette Children's Hospital had a great little stage, so we decided to host a show for all of the kids in the place.

After we received permission from the powers that be, the show was a go. It consisted of re-creating an old radio show (a lifelong interest of mine) complete with sound effects; a shameless rip-off of the Johnny Carson character, Carnac the Magnificent; and some pretty darn good music. A friend had a band called Free and Easy. It was a large band, and the guys had a terrific sense of fun, involving themselves in all aspects of the show. The production was completed by a local pizzeria donating food for everybody. An evening to remember, many years after the laughs, giggles, and music have faded into the night.

Someone contacted Gary Hebert, a well-loved reporter at the *St. Paul Pioneer Press,* about the event. One evening, a call came in. "I'd like to do a story on the group. What do you call yourselves?"

I hadn't thought about that. Thinking fast now, the only thing I could come up with was "Duck Soup Players." Having watched an old Marx brothers movie, *Duck Soup,* the night before, it was the only name I could think of.

Gary said, "Like the old Marx brothers, huh? It's a catchy name for a theater company. I like it!" That name would stick for the next forty-some years. Within a couple of days after the story ran, the phone was ringing with requests for shows at senior residences. What to do? I had just blurted out that Duck Soup thing, not thinking about the consequences. We really weren't an organized group set up to do such a tour. Rallying friends together who shared the common cause, Duck Soup Players was formed for real. The band couldn't stay on as they traveled a lot, but the others were committed. We had to act fast to live up to that article with its embellishments. We scheduled performances a couple of months ahead without having anything that resembled a show.

Someone gave us a short, fun radio script from the University of Minnesota radio station. We reworked it quickly into something for a stage presentation. Pete Brueggeman put the talent he learned from his cabinet-making father to excellent use, building a set, props, and a curtain system. Tom Monson had similar talents and, like Pete, enjoyed the technical end of theater, though Tom also had an artistic flair for music, acting, and costumes. Duck Soup was lucky to have these guys on board. I doubt if we would have survived without them and their dedication. They stayed on with the players for a very long time, especially Pete with twenty-eight years of service, until health issues caught up with him.

We rounded up other friends to take parts and started rehearsals, and unbelievably, we did it! The show was a hit with seniors, and we never looked back. Word spread, and demand for Duck Soup has never ceased.

At first we paid for everything ourselves to make the shows physically possible. But as the productions grew in sophistication, in terms of sets, scripts, technical abilities, and demand for performances, it became too much for us financially. In the late 1970s, Duck Soup Players put an "Inc." after the name and we became an official nonprofit organization. It was now officially a 501(c)(3) and eligible to receive donations. That was made easier by the fact that we had a track record and the media liked us. Columnist Gary Hebert did a piece on us every year with an occasional feature thrown in. Corporate funding increased with an angel or two joining our list of supporters as well.

Managing the company as well as acting became my full-time job. More newspapers and television stations were interested in the mission of Duck Soup. U.S. Senator Boshwitz from Minnesota picked us up on his radar screen, mentioning us to the USO in Washington, D.C., which sent a person to check out our current show on the circuit. It was "The Golden Age of Radio." This show was a collection of music, comedy scripts, and commercials from the 1930s and 1940s. The cast was enormously talented. The USO wasted no time booking us for a tour of VA hospitals for the spring of 1980. I think the tour was designed to test us. They scheduled thirty-three performances in twenty-one days in eighteen cities between Minneapolis and the East Coast, including a performance in the middle of the Pentagon. WOW! It was tough, but the positive reaction was huge. The Pentagon wanted to sign us up through the USO for another tour, this time of remote military stations in Alaska for that fall. At first I balked, "Golden Age for guys in their late teens or early twenties? I don't think it'll work. Let us put something else together."

The USO representative said, "Just give it a try. Believe me, they will love it!"

They did! Various commanders called the Duck Soup Players the best unit ever to tour Alaska. Whew, heady stuff! It was to be the second of seven USO tours, two to Alaska and five to VA hospitals from Maine to California.

During all this USO business, we still had to maintain our mission at home. I am forever indebted to Pete Brueggeman for helping put a second company together and managing it while the other team was on the road. Then one day a very tidy envelope arrived. You'll find arriving envelopes to be a recurring theme in this book.

The return address was the White House. I thought it was a joke at first, but then I opened the card and it read, "In honor of the President and Mrs. Reagan, Bob Hope and his friends request the honor of your company at A Salute to the USO on the occasion of its Fortieth Anniversary, Saturday evening, the Seventeenth of October 1981."

I about fell over. By inviting us to this event, the powers on high were recognizing our mission and our body of work. Pete Brueggeman was just the man to bring along. Having missed going on all but one of the USO tours because of his home-front dedication, he deserved it. All of the living presidents were invited. Presidents Reagan and Ford, Bob Hope, dignitaries, military brass, Hollywood entertainers, and network personalities rounded out the guest list. Oh, yes, there were the two of us Duck Soupers from fly-over land. You just had to know it would be us that caused a bit of a fuss to kick off the evening.

Pete set off the alarms as we entered the gala. This was just five months after President Reagan had been shot. I'm sure the Secret Service was on high alert as they grabbed poor Pete aside. They were courteous, mind you, but not about to take any chances. After some fancy wand waving and Pete showing them his doctor-issued implant card (he has implanted hips and knees), they let us pass.

The second surprise was on us. Of all the funny people in the room that night including Bob Hope, it was President Ford who had us splitting our sides laughing as he regaled the audience with his golfing adventures. He certainly wasn't afraid to laugh at himself. How cool was that?

Back to my reality, I began to reflect on a common thread no matter where we performed. The elderly in senior housing, hospitalized kids, lonely soldiers far from home, and those in VA hospitals—they craved a sense of normalcy in daily life. So many of these people missed their pets deeply.

By the early 1990s, I was ready to do something about it, at least in our metro area. I bought Katie, a Rottweiler, as a puppy. She was raised, trained, and socialized to be my companion and a therapy dog—a job she excelled at to an incredible degree. We worked three assisted living residences. Katie knew the names of her favorite people and which apartments were theirs. Our pet therapy program became a wing of the Duck Soup Players. It was more successful than my highest expectations, garnering high praise and more friendly media coverage. The demand for time with Katie far outstripped my ability to deliver a bit of furry love. The problem was that we didn't have enough therapy dogs to go around. The concept, from my perspective, hadn't really caught on to the degree it had by the time Ruby set paw into a facility years later.

Luckily, the administrators in the facilities where Ruby started her new career in late November 2005 did not have any concern about her looking like a pit bull. There was the formal interview process, background checks, rules, regulations, and procedures review that every therapy dog and handler must go through. That was it. Ruby was already tested and certified and carried the hefty insurance policy all therapy dogs did. They had no breed prejudice. A few employees and some family members who expressed concern at first were soon converted, singing praises as they saw little Ruby work that kind magic on the seniors.

Bob and Millie, the magic couple, as I called them, were typical of the other residents in that their marriage endured a lifetime. The difference was that they were both still together deep into their eighties. Millie was bedridden, very frail, but her mind was like a steel trap—sharp, clear, and nimble, with total recall of past and current events. Her husband, Bob, being able-bodied, lived in an apartment across the street, but joined Millie early in the morning every day. He'd spend the day tending to her needs and comfort, though she asked for little and never complained about her health in those twilight years. What she did crave was spirited conversation, even debate, and Bob was up to the task, staying late into the evening every day without fail. The one luxury they allowed themselves was a "nice" radio. They'd listen to the Minnesota Twins, but much rather enjoyed minor league ball. News events, public radio, and newspapers called for analysis. I never saw them watch television. There it sat, screen empty and black. Think they were on to something?

It was into this awe-inspiring relationship that Ruby and I were welcomed with open arms. Bob and Millie were dog people of the first order. They loved to have Ruby share Millie's bed. Gingerly, Ruby would pick out just the right spot and carefully lay within easy reach of Millie's gentle hand, tail thumping the blankets.

In the coming days, weeks, and months, I learned that this incredible couple didn't come from academia backgrounds as I had imagined. Bob had worked for the railroad from the Great Depression years through World War II and to his retirement. Millie had been a housewife. It was obvious that they respected each other enormously. He loved his wife's sharp intelligence. We talked about the depression, the dogs they used to have, and Bob's work. They recounted the worry and fears of the war years and the pride in their children and grandchildren. Vacation adventures from the 1940s and 1950s were retold with finite detail, making for stories rich in texture and color.

They told Ruby, as she listened to every word, and me about their honeymoon. Bob had a new Plymouth, which was a big deal in the late 1930s. Millie, having never driven a car, asked Bob for a turn at the wheel. "Sure, dear." His bride promptly smacked up the Plymouth. There was no major damage to the car and only minor bruising to the happy couple. Instead of anger, Bob simply took the time to teach Millie the finer points of vehicle operation.

Ruby and I usually stayed longer than our schedule called for; it was always so hard to leave. Before we left, Millie always asked for and received a Ruby kiss, making us promise to return soon. Millie would sometimes say, "It feels so good when Ruby lies next to me. I'm always so cold, and she puts out a lot of heat."

As we arrived one morning for rounds, the staff informed us of Millie's death with Bob at her side. I felt terrible and sad, and then I thought about poor Bob and the loss of his beloved best friend. I knew he had to be devastated. I told the supervisor I was going to go to Bob's apartment to extend our condolences, but she said he had left town to stay with his son's family for a while. We never saw him again, never had a chance to say good-bye and thank him for sharing their lives with Ruby and myself. Losing someone you really like all too quickly is a downside of the job, I suppose. I sure didn't like it.

Another one of the first residents Ruby befriended was Hank. Hank wasn't able to talk, his body wracked with terminal cancer. Even though he was in excruciating pain, his eyes said everything we had to know. When Ruby entered the room, he would flash a great smile of a man years younger. His eyes, bright, clear, and shining, danced all over Ruby as she took up a position alongside him. After a quick slurp of a kiss that had him giggling, she'd snuggle up tight to the kind old gentleman with those expressive eyes. I'd narrate any interesting stories about Ruby's day or things planned in the near future. Hank would nod at my ramblings as he slowly, tenderly stroked her head and back. He seemed to be reminiscing of long ago pets. Suddenly his eyes grew dull as they closed; his body shuddered in pain. A couple of minutes later, Hank was back, petting Ruby. He'd frequently glance at me, silently saying thank you for bringing Ruby. The pain returned twice more. He was tiring. It was time for us to go and let him rest. It was a hard day when some months later Ruby and I learned of Hank's passing, alone in his room.

Ruby and I have had the honor of being privy to many residents' life stories, an America long passed. We shared accountings from the 1930s, '40s, and '50s and the history-changing events of those years, each told from a different perspective. Some did fairly well during the Great Depression. Others struggled desperately. During World War II, millions of men went off to battle and some, like Bob, worked on the home front. Women took nice-paying factory jobs in the war effort only to lose them as the men returned home. Being a history buff, I have certainly read about these things. But coming from real living people makes for an infinitely fascinating fabric of time. Ruby's work never got boring. The common thread with the seniors, of course, was Ruby herself. She was the trigger for most conversations. I'd been told by staff that some residents who hardly ever opened up and talked made amazing transformations when Ruby visited. That kind of statement would not be news to the many volunteers and their therapy dogs as they made a difference in seniors' lives across America.

Another upside of her therapy work was that the adult children of Ruby's residents saw the wonderful role she played in the lives of their parents. Through the years, some of these adult children, wanting to do something positive for themselves and others, went on to train therapy dogs of their very own.

Ruby not only continues to visit seniors on a regular schedule, but also calls on schools to talk about dog safety, the different breeds of dogs, and the many ways dogs help people.

Along the way, she has taken a bump or two. During a pet

therapy session at a memory care unit, a staffer asked if Ruby could see Mrs. Smith. "Oh, her kids say she's always been a dog person. She just loves them!" As Ruby said hi, wack! She was socked in the face. The problem was that Mrs. Smith was a resident here because she was not the same Mrs. Smith anymore. It is a difficult reality for many grown children to deal with their moms or dads who are in effect gone. Ruby stepped back, looking at me as if to say, "What was that, Dad? What do I do?" Snapping out of my shock, I whisked Ruby out of harm's way. The staff was mortified. While I wasn't happy about Ruby getting punched by poor Mrs. Smith, I couldn't be angry with her. If Mrs. Smith had been aware of what she had done, she would have been mortified as well. Ruby was all right and, yes, we went back. Ruby wouldn't have it any other way.

Chapter Five

My Katrina Cajun Queen…A Love Lost

A friend of ours went to New Orleans after Hurricane Katrina as a volunteer with a Minnesota animal rescue group. She returned shaken by the images of total devastation and a pit bull the group deemed too dog aggressive. The rescue group wanted nothing to do with the dog that had been named Molly. They would not pay for any care, food, or medicine—nothing!

Our friend was told that if she brought the dog back to Minnesota, it would be her responsibility. Once again, we were called upon as the couple who helped desperate dogs of this breed. And just like the final call asking us to take Ruby for that Thanksgiving weekend, we were asked to take in Molly for a short while. Lynn and I agreed to foster Molly. Like Tiger, Molly's ears were cropped to the skull. She had heart worms, whip worms, and hook worms, was anemic, had badly burned feet, and had a healing cut on her body. But most troubling were numerous old scars. Molly had recently had puppies, the doctor said. She seemed to have had a hard life and acted like it; of course, the trauma of Katrina must also be factored into the equation.

Though Molly showed aggression toward dogs, she showed no aggression toward people. But she didn't seem to understand kindness. She was too timid to show a lot of affection, but the ensuing months brought her good health and unbounded happiness—even excitement for snow! Many peaceful hours were spent with Molly in my lap, head on my chest, being stroked by "kind hands" as we would say aloud.

Molly was making slow progress with accepting the other dogs, but it was Ruby's calm, respectful, nonthreatening behavior that really began to work wonders in changing Molly's attitude toward the other members of our "tribe." She had a comfy apartment in my office above the garage. Molly's life was on the mend.

But one day, it all started to come apart. People came forward claiming Molly as theirs. That was fine, but we had questions. We certainly did not want her going to the wrong family or to an abusive family.

A phone call was arranged. The person on the other end of the line started out defiant and threatening. "What's the dog's name?" we asked. Molly didn't respond to the name given. "When did she have puppies?"

"Don't know, maybe two years ago." This was the wrong answer according to the vet.

"What about the old scars?"

"Oh, ahhh, something fell on her."

At the end of the call, I said this just didn't sound like your dog. With that, things turned ugly.

"We paid $15,000 for that dog!" A few minutes later, it was $5,000. They said they would come up to Minnesota, find us, and beat up my family members and me. It was time to hang up.

A firestorm followed. The rescue group who wanted nothing to do with Molly suddenly wanted her back. Apparently the family who wanted Molly threatened to take the rescue group to court. Paperwork suddenly materialized saying Molly was in their charge.

We dug in. The shelter, who had no idea who we were, began a smear campaign against us. We were called racists, thieves, and more. It was a terrible time.

Yes, we loved Molly, but if the true, caring family was found then it was time for her to go home. With these people who now claimed Molly, we had questions, but their answers did not add up and kept changing. In the end, the rescue shelter got us.

Lynn and I were in the process of adopting a little girl from China. The shelter moved into high gear, having the sheriff send us an email followed by a phone call telling us we would be arrested and charged for having stolen property. Our squeaky-clean record needed to stay that way for the adoption to go through.

So, they won. Dear sweet Molly had to go. On a cold, wintery Saturday morning, our friend placed Molly on the seat of her truck. Molly stared into my face, her eyes searching, confused. I should have turned away perhaps, but I couldn't. I just looked back into her eyes, speechless. That moment will remain with me all my live-long days.

Later, friends suggested I should have let Molly "run away" to a safe location. I guess I was gutless. I hadn't even thought of it at the time. In due course, we heard Molly's family complained that she was too aggressive toward their other new dogs. Then, there was nothing. I dare not think about what happened to her.

We know our hearts were in the right place for Molly. All we wanted was the best for her, as we do for all of our foster dogs. Over the years, we have had many wonderful, heartwarming experiences fostering dogs, with Ruby at the pinnacle. This Katrina nightmare left us shaken to our inner cores. For awhile afterward, we even questioned why we did what we did with rescue work. That thought didn't last too long, however, when on a quiet evening Ruby gently rested her head on my lap. Our eyes met and, I thought "No life should be wasted."

CHAPTER SIX

It's Showtime! Ruby on Radio and Stage

In December 2005, Ruby, bored, decided she wanted something else to do besides lounging around the house napping, snacking, and wandering aimlessly from room to room.

"I'll go to work with Dad at the radio station. Fun! Some action!"

And so she did, where the girl carried on the napping, snacking, and wandering aimlessly from room to room. Luckily, my boss, a dog lover, allowed her to stay on. Two days later, Ruby was running the place, i.e., everyone in the building fawning over her to the point of some serious weight gain in just a few weeks.

They weren't all lazy, food-filled days. Ruby excelled at greeting my in-studio guests. "Pat's Pot Luck" consisted of a little talk, a little music, and guest interviews with the local mayor, congresswoman Michele Bachmann, the head of the Better Business Bureau, law enforcement officers, Adam West, chefs, and more. It didn't matter to Ruby. She usually curled up on her chair next to the guest, or for some unknown reason, she'd sleep on the floor, head draped over their feet. We wondered if it was a comment on our subject matter. Ruby would also, from time to time, start snoring, getting progressively louder. And yes, it was picked up by the microphones to the bemusement of Jess, my engineer; Kim, the office manager; and listeners. Enough was enough! I'd quietly reach over the board with a yardstick, gently poking Ruby in the ribs until she'd stir or stop the window rattling.

During one interview, Ruby's snoring was particularly embarrassing. A Republican congresswoman was our guest that day, and her message was certainly on the serious side. Ruby demonstrated that she was either a Democrat or independent, snoring lightly at times, increasing the decibel level as the congresswoman became more passionate about her message. The yardstick received quite a workout that day. Unprofessional? Er, yes. Congresswoman angry or upset? No! She was very fleet of foot using the fact that she was a dog person with Ruby curled up next to her and would work hard to get Ruby's vote. Luckily my boss, dog lover that he was, didn't hear the broadcast. We had crossed the line, and I knew it. But Ruby was entitled to her opinion, I suppose.

When a guest was not a dog person, Ruby was banished to the office where she still had a clear view of the goings on in the studio through a large window separating the rooms. As the guest sat down, Ruby would give me a look as if to say, "But, but I'm supposed to be in there taking care of things!" When it was apparent she wasn't joining us, I received one more look…a dirty scowl. Then she just curled up and took a fitful nap.

One guest in particular was absolutely fascinating—Adnan Bin Abdulkareem Ahmed Alkaissey El Farthie, who is better known in the professional wrestling world as "Sheikh Adnan Alkaissey." He was my guest twice. We talked about his book *The Sheikh of Baghdad*, an interestingly written book that was a thrilling read. We discussed when he and Saddam Hussein were friends, teenagers hanging out in Baghdad coffee shops. Saddam, tall, lanky, well dressed, and polite, always had a newspaper or book at hand. Anxious to talk

Middle East politics, Saddam was intrigued by the young, up-and-coming, increasingly influential Baath party. A young Adnan could see Saddam had a destiny.

Meanwhile, Adnan Alkaissey, who was allowed to use the title "Sheikh" because his father was the Imam, or spiritual leader, of the Almahdia Mosque in Baghdad, wanted to spread his wings and travel to see the world. Because he excelled in sports, especially amateur wrestling, he wanted to come to America via the American Friends of the Middle East on a football scholarship. Adnan loved America, the freedom, and the people. He stayed and went on to become a huge success in professional wrestling.

Then in 1969, Alkaissey was visiting family in Iraq. Adnan was "asked" by Saddam, now chairman of the powerful Revolutionary Command Council, to do his wrestling at home, in his birthplace. Adnan had made a big name for himself in America so Saddam reasoned that the Sheikh owed it to his fellow countrymen to show them that they could be successful. Saddam wanted an Arab champion whose struggles could reflect those of the Baath party. Saddam "asked" again. Adnan simply could not refuse his old friend and was appointed Saddam's general director of youth at the Youth Ministry. He became an Arab champion in Iraq and the Middle East. Adnan became rich and a cultural icon performing in front of hundreds of thousands of screaming, cheering fans.

Saddam meanwhile, had been using him as a PR tool to divert attention from his real plans, but Adnan became too rich and too popular, to the chagrin of Hussein, who finally decided he had to go. Adnan dodged a car bomb that left him badly shaken. Leaving millions in the bank (Saddam's version of the Gestapo report would report any large withdrawals), he escaped over the Kuwait border in the dead of night with just a few grand in his pocket. Back in America, as an American citizen, Adnan lived the American dream, picking up his career as a pro wrestler.

How odd it was to look at pictures of him as a young man sitting at a news conference with Saddam Hussein, and now sitting across from me with Ruby fast asleep on his feet.

———

By the summer of 2006, Ruby and I were looking for more fun adventures when Lynn noticed an audition notice for a dog in *Cheaper by the Dozen* at Lakeshore Players, a well-respected community theater located northeast of Minneapolis. On the night of auditions, Ruby was on her back in the middle of seventy-five to one hundred auditioning kids enjoying every minute! Alas, she was not cast, we suspect by the looks we were given by some of the adults, because of her breed. That's okay, we had a vacation planned and now wouldn't have to change those plans. Ruby would put her acting career on hold.

About a week before we were to leave on our trip, the phone rang. The person asked whether Ruby was still available.

"Sure!" I said, without checking with Lynn first.

Big mistake! After much, "Gee, Patrick, honey, we're leaving on our trip next week. Golly, it certainly would have been nice if we had talked it over before you said yes."

In reality, it didn't go quite that smoothly, but Lynn did see the good in it, for Ruby, for the breed, and yes, even for me. (She just couldn't resist my excitement.)

But now, precious weeks of rehearsal had been lost. There were only about two weeks before opening night for Ruby. Arriving at the theater for the first rehearsal, we were told by some cast members that the dog who had been originally cast, while nice, was a bit unruly. The kids took to Ruby immediately. Adult cast members as a whole accepted her as well. Some of the parents were clearly concerned about the prospect of their children spending night after night rehearsing and then four weekends of performing with a pit bull. By opening night, however, the happy, calm little dog had won everyone's hearts as parents and kids requested getting their pictures taken with Ruby!

The dressing rooms, green room, and reception area were all located in the basement of the theater. As just before any production opener, there was an absolute flurry of activity with costumes rechecked, repaired, and fitted and props carefully gone over. In the middle of the buzz with kids running back and forth, no one noticed the stranger standing at the end of the hall, no one except Ruby, that is. She had been lying on the floor in the middle of the hub-bub.

As for me, I was lounging in a chair off to the side unable to see down the hall. But watching Ruby rise slowly, smoothly, as if she had hydraulic legs caught my attention. Scrambling to my feet, I had never before seen this behavior in Ruby. I barely had taken a step toward her when she took two stiff-legged advances of her own toward the interloper, head down, letting go of a low, menacing growl, glancing quickly at me, then back at the suspect. My pace quickened, and then I saw him. A guy wearing a dark sweatshirt and baseball cap with his head lowered as if in a staredown with Ruby. Seeing me, he looked for a second and turned to exit up the stairs and out the side door.

That was the first and only time I saw Ruby display a posturing attitude. When the man disappeared, Ruby looked up into my eyes with her tail wagging as if to say, "Did I do okay, Dad?" You did great, kid!

Every stage show in America, whether professional or community theater, has a final dress rehearsal, last tech night, or preview night. Call it what you will, but it's the night before the official opening. It's the last chance to work out any bugs that need attention in lighting, tech, cues, costumes, props, the set's working pieces, and the like. In most cases, an audience of friends or family is invited. It really helps the cast and crew with timing. I, by this time, was increasingly becoming Ruby's manservant and bodyguard. So, luckily, I didn't have a part in this production. I simply had to hand off Ruby to the boy and girl who made their entrance from the second floor hall and stepped lively down the stairs into the living room. Tonight, there was magic and excitement in the air. Ruby felt it big time. She was totally pumped from the surrounding energy and loving every minute of it. Then it struck me. She was one of them. One of the cast, and she seemed to know it! "Thanks, Dad. I'm ready." How strange it seemed. Thirty-six years in theater and I would not be going out on stage tonight, but how wonderful it was to let Ruby carry the torch. Non-pet owners will no doubt blanch at this, but it was like seeing your kid go out there.

"You're on! Go!" the stage manager whispered, breaking every emotional thought. Now my thought was, "God help us!" During rehearsals, the kids bounded down the stairs with Ruby on a leash and I had just one thing to worry about…the kids being pulled down the stairs too fast and falling, bouncing their little chins off of every step. But tonight there was a whole new set of concerns. Someone had the bright idea to just let Ruby run down the steps without the leash and when she got to the bottom, the other kids off to the right would call her to the couch. She certainly couldn't resist.

Not able to see a thing, I held my breath, listening intently. Kids scrambling down steps…sounds good. The audience said, "Awww,"…sounds even better. Then laughter erupted. Wait! There's not supposed to be laughter. More laughter. Oh! Oh! Then howls of laughter. Oh, shoot! Then it was obvious the audience couldn't contain itself.

"What's going on?" I screamed in a whisper.

"I can't see a thing," came back from some disembodied voice. For a big guy, I could move pretty fast on occasion. This was one of them! I blasted down the backstage stairs, raced across the reception area, up the side stairs of the theater, and peeked out the door onto the stage. There was Ruby on the couch with a gaggle of kids. Right where she's supposed to be!

So what had happened? Ruby, in all her happy excitement, had "lost" it for a moment. Reaching the main stage, she skittered once around the set, leapt off stage left, over the orchestra pit, raced up the aisle to the back of the theater, crossed over to the right aisle, tore back to the stage hitting her mark on the couch with the kids! After that, a leash was used in every performance!

For us, opening night would be highlighted by Lee's Limos donating a ride for Ruby to the theater complete with a red carpet. The media was notified about a rescue dog's rags-to-riches story, but nobody showed up. It was still great fun with lots of people wondering, "What in the world?"

After Ruby arrived at the theater, Mary, the limo driver, graciously offered to take the kids for a quick ride with Ruby. Again I stayed back. These were good kids and didn't need my supervision. Ruby, for her part, I heard later, gave the kids a tour of the limo. Up on the seats, down off the seats, up on the seats. "Hey," she seemed to say, "look at this cool ice bucket. Oh I love to crunch the ice," as she gingerly picked an ice cube and chomped, then another one as if to offer it to the kids. Even though they loved Ruby, the kids declined.

Enduring friendships are many times forged during a theatrical production. This was no exception. Katie, the little ten-year-old girl Ruby had a scene with, weighed in at forty-three pounds, ten pounds lighter than her four-legged co-star. In a touching scene, Katie held Ruby's face in her tiny hands, asking why she couldn't behave. Ruby gazed back unmoving, steady, calm. At the end of the pleading, Ruby gave Katie one kiss right on cue. A warm "awww" from the audience always followed. They loved it! Night after night, the scene went without a hitch. (Yes!)

Katie was an enormously talented child with a great natural affinity for dogs. Seeing such terrific abilities in her, I seized the moment to cast her in a number of Duck Soup Players productions. Three years later, people still asked, "When will that girl who was so good be on your stage again?" Not for a while, I'm afraid. She moved on to the Minneapolis Children's Theater and television commercials both local and national. But the friendship lasted, and when she saw Ruby on occasion, Katie repeated the scene they played in *Cheaper by the Dozen*, and Ruby still gave her the kiss right on cue.

In putting a community theater production together, you can usually count on coming up with a cast of widely diverse backgrounds. Their reasons for involvement are varied as well. They hopefully have a degree of talent, which also comes in a wide spectrum. Some have regular day jobs but have a bit of a Walter Mitty complex. Some are students who may have dreams of making it big one day. Others might be lonely, have troubles at home, have high-pressure jobs and need an outlet. But the bottom line is, they all have a love of the theater, the crowds, the camaraderie, the smell of the greasepaint, and a chance at more dating material. *Cheaper by the Dozen* certainly had many of these elements.

I talked earlier about forging new friendships during a show as with Ruby and Katie, and so too was it for a couple of cast members and myself. J.P. Barone was a man in distress. As an assistant state attorney general, he always had a full plate. Add to that his beloved father's rapidly deteriorating health, and you have someone who could use an outlet. A veteran of many shows, J.P. was cast, ironically, as a dying father to twelve kids in *Cheaper by the Dozen*. (The name is the only thing in common with the recent movies.) Still, J.P. is affable, fun, and interesting. He knows more about pre-1975 movies than anyone this side of a computer...directors, marriages, locations, set designers, and stars.

He also out-did Jim Backus when it came to playing a well-moneyed snob. Though no snob in real life, he did have an air of class and distinction and was a swell dresser. Boy, he knew his Armani suits. We also suspected he cut his lawn in a nicely filled jacket.

Close to opening night, his dad's health was getting worse; J.P. would get up very early in the morning and drive 250 miles to visit his father briefly and return, driving another 250 miles. He was committed to his dad, but as the lead, he had a lot of people depending on him.

On preview night, J.P. knew the time was nearing the end for his father. He had just returned from that round trip in the rain barely in time to dress for the show. J.P. badly needed a smile that night. His dad had less than twenty-four hours to live. I didn't know it for several years, but Ruby, with her wild excursions off stage around the theater and back up again, gave J.P. what he needed most—a smile, a chuckle, and a laugh, seeing a life lived to the fullest, the perfect prescription for a person in need.

Jack Rhodes was another fellow in the show with an interesting day job, coincidentally in law enforcement as the chief of staff of a county prosecutor's office. He, too, had stresses and obligations in his position. Like J.P., Jack was kind of "GQ," but a tad more on the casual side, in manner and dress. Theater and motorcycles were his prescription for relief. Mr. Rhodes was married to a television reporter and a cop. (No, not two wives!) He had been in the Peace Corps, and was a writer and newspaper editor, not to mention that his college years were fodder for a book just waiting to be written.

J.P., Jack, Ruby, and I remained friends over the years, going on to do other productions together, some including Ruby. Ruby and I stopped by Jack's downtown office often, and we would have lunch, coffee, and chew the fat. We had visited so often, in fact, that the security people greeted us with "Hi, Ruby, how are you?" The veterans would tell the newbies all about the great things the four-legged guest has done. "Saw you on TV, honey!" Then they directed their attention to me. "Sir, could you please empty your pockets and step through here?" It's okay, though—it's all positive. Upstairs, Ruby met county attorney Susan Gaertner numerous times. (She even had a pittie in the family.) Susan gave speeches around the country on the relationship of cruelty to animals to spousal abuse, child abuse, and murder. Ruby and I received a letter from Ms. Gaertner in appreciation of Ruby's work in the community and the fact that she believes it is the owner and not the breed that is the cause of the problems. On reading that, Ruby gave me that faint Mona Lisa look and I thought I heard her say, "Heh, heh, think I'll run for office one of these years."

CHAPTER SEVEN

Life on the Dusty Trail … Fun-Filled
Family Vacations?

"You people are crazy! Six dogs in a motor home?!"

If you've seen ex-reality TV stars the Goslins traveling with their eight kids, you're reminded of a mini-military operation. To those traveling with multiple dogs in a motor home, it's nothing new. It's certainly easier.

But for Lynn and me, the challenges were different. Vacationing with a family of Rottweilers and pit bulls, we could forget about hotels. (We tried that just once, but more about that later.) It's not just a matter of tossing the dogs into a dumpy motor home and bouncing down the road with the idea that everyone will think, "Awww, isn't that cute." We had better have them well trained and socialized with ourselves established as pack leaders. Believe us, we would be dealing with public perception and fear. There was no room for untrained hooligans.

We had experienced prejudice close to home earlier. It is certainly no different on the road. Everything we did, said, wore, and drove, and our and the dogs' behaviors, would all be up for scrutiny. If we were to use these dogs as ambassadors, it would be best not to get into people's faces. Let them be curious and come to you.

For years, we'd visit a particular KOA campground in the Dakotas. The manager, to his credit, was always cordial, but kept a close eye on us. Then it finally happened. Lynn and I were outside at the campsite, lounging, reading, and enjoying a sweet summer afternoon when the manager walked by, stopped, and looked at the dogs. Ruby and Katie, on leashes, barely moved their heads. He continued to watch us to the point of being somewhat uncomfortable.

Oh man, he's going to ask us to leave and we haven't done anything wrong, I thought.

Finally, he spoke, "I really can't believe how well behaved your dogs are. It's so nice to see these kinds of dogs owned by responsible people. I wish more owners were like you. Over the years, we've had to ask people with all kinds of dogs with behavior problems to leave. But people are always afraid of those kinds. (Oh, I just love it when people say "those kinds.") Many KOAs won't let you in no matter what. If you've got a $2 million rig or an older unit, if you have those kinds, you can't stay because their insurance companies say no. I go through a different insurer than most and have had no problems so far. But you people are making a good point!"

I nearly leapt up and kissed the guy on the lips! I casually replied, "Thanks, sir, for noticing. We appreciate it."

With that he said, "No problem." He gave a smile and a quick nod and walked on.

Cesar Millan, the dog whisperer, had it so right when he said, "You must be the ultimate pack leader. There must be rules, boundaries, and limitations."

Whether it's at home or vacationing, when you have dogs, particularly dogs of this size and power, you better have control. If not, it could spell big trouble for you, the dogs, and the breeds whose tarnished image you're trying to improve, not to mention the poor soul your beloved pet may be intimidating. It's training, training, training, and socializing, socializing, and socializing. Be smart about it. Prepare for travel. There are always different environments, strange people, animals, smells, and unexpected events that will be much easier to deal with if you're ready for them. None of this is rocket science...just common sense.

When we would stop for a potty break, a sightseeing moment, or a dinner out, we were always peppered with questions: "How do you do it?" Followed by, "Isn't it way too much work?" And occasionally, "What have they done to the inside of your motor home?" We're happy to report that the interior of our bewheeled vacation home is free of rips, tears, chew marks, or mistake spots. And actually, no, it isn't too much work.

At first there was a lot of fuss in getting the routine down. A few short weekend jaunts were in order. We were all adjusting, but things did fall into place. Our kids had their favorite spots to ride. Occasionally, they quietly swapped positions. Once in a while, several of them, for example Carla, Ruby, and Molly, would claim the same spot at the same time. No problem. They would simply pile on top of each other like rugby players.

Each knew where their personal feeding station was located. Thank goodness we didn't have to deal with food aggression!

At night, same thing, everybody had a spot—Ruby in bed, Venus and Carla on the couch, and Tiger and Molly in dog beds on the floor. Potty breaks followed a pecking order. If we decided to mix it up a little, they looked at us as if we had three heads. The routine really did become natural. Like breathing, we didn't even have to think about it.

None of this is to say it was a well-oiled machine every minute of every mile. There were issues such as the errant buffalo plodding through our Yellowstone campsite one frosty June morning snorting, puffing, and stomping his front hooves. He was a magnificent beast.

Inside the camper, things were quiet, every eye trained on this interloper. One last snort from the buffalo, and Tiger had enough. An angry bark set off holy hell with everybody barking, even Ruby with that little gruff voice! They jumped from window to window, snapping at each other as the buffalo, duly unimpressed, sauntered on.

Why is it that when facing a common enemy, pack members sometimes turn on each other? "I'll take care of this." Another would pipe in, "No, it's my job!" "No, I'm bigger." Still another, "It's your fault for letting that thing get too close." It just makes no sense! Either way, we were shaken. Everyone in the campground must have heard the ruckus, all that dog training shot to pieces.

Then there were times when their behavior left us completely stumped. One evening in Idaho as dusk was settling in, we pulled into a rest stop so Lynn could use a land-line phone to check in back home. As usual, Tiger took Lynn's seat at about the same time she hopped out. Because Lynn was the alpha female, her seat was valuable real estate! Casually slumped in his newly acquired position, Tiger, relaxed, kept watch over Lynn. But in a heartbeat, he was on full alert puffing himself up, making a strange guttural crying sound as he zeroed in on a character I wouldn't have picked up even in the good old days of hitchhiking.

He was between thirty and forty years old, with hair that reminded me of the '60s wrestler "Wild Man of Borneo." Filthy clothes, unshaven, and just plain unsavory, he approached the phone next to Lynn checking for forgotten change. My hand tightened on the door handle, ready to spring. Finding no change, he looked around, and didn't even give our motor home a hard glance. He positioned himself closer to Lynn.

That's it! I'm out of here! A loud blast, a sharp pain in my right ear, stopped me short. The side glass shook, and I felt the door handle vibrate. It was Tiger letting out a bellowing rant that stiffened the hairs on the back of my neck. This soft-eyed, peace-loving rescue dog with no ears and an unsteady gate was putting it on the line. I had no doubt Tiger would lay down his life for us. The shadowy man took notice of the camper, this time with eyes as big as saucers. He wheeled away from Lynn beelining it through the trees toward the other side of the rest stop.

Squeezing my 250-pound frame through the smallest possible door opening so Tiger wouldn't follow, I trotted over to Lynn. With her head down, engrossed in conversation, she hadn't noticed or paid any attention to the stranger until Tiger's violent outburst.

Tiger was still swearing, telling the unseen culprit exactly what he'd do to him if he hurt us. Then it hit me—nobody else was barking. They were watching intently, but not a sound. Again, it didn't make sense. I'm not complaining, mind you. Was it some unseen communication to the other dogs? A tone? Whatever it was, it worked! There they were, sitting tall and erect behind "Mr. T" like Catholic schoolgirls ready to sing a song for the cardinal.

Entering the motor home, Lynn was greeted with much tumult, tail wagging, kisses, sniffing, and close body contact. Ascertaining that she was okay, it was every dog for themselves to find a comfortable place to sprawl out for a well-deserved nap. Up until now, Ruby was looking down on all the activity from her perch on a club chair. She hopped down, gave Lynn a quick once over, looked up with an approving few tail wags, zipped back to her throne, and flopped down fast asleep. Ruby hadn't ascended to alpha yet, but she was acting more like it.

We didn't know what the stranger's motives were that evening or what would have happened if Lynn had been traveling alone. It was a valuable firsthand lesson to stay vigilant when engrossed in some activity like making a phone call, working an ATM, or having car trouble. Tiger would not always be there to save the day.

———

It was a hot, sticky Midwestern night around 11 p.m. Our July vacation had gotten off to a late start due to some tire problems that delayed our departure from the Twin Cities by hours. But now we were on our way to Yellowstone National Park.

Growing up in this part of the country, we should have known there was trouble ahead when the air was hot, thick, heavy, and moisture-laden with a deathly stillness. At least I should have known. But we were too excited to be on our way at last! Besides, it was cool and comfortable in the motor home. Lynn had taken over driving, while I relaxed at the dinette with a good book, a couple of homemade rice crispy bars, and a cup of freshly brewed coffee. The hum of the generator in the distance, cool zephyrs of air caressing my body, a light clickity-clack of tar strips on the road under the tires reminded me of a train. It was all very hypnotic and relaxing.

The dogs, meanwhile, were in deep slumber. Ruby and Tiger, on occasion with their snoring, attempted to do renditions of popular show tunes. It made for some fun giggles. Yes, all was right with the world. Then as we approached Sioux Falls, South Dakota, from the east, Lynn noticed heavy lightning in the distance ahead. "Hon, look at that! Cool! Ooooooh, ahhhh."

I switched off my reading light, sitting in the dark as we entered Mother Nature's theater, ready for the light show. We didn't have to wait long. Bang! It was on us! The lightning was constant, giving us a clear view of the horrible madness in the clouds. Before we could say anything to each other, we were nailed! Wind and rain hit us as hard as a freight train. In a heartbeat, Lynn couldn't see the road ahead at sixty miles per hour! The wind decided it didn't want us on the road at all, giving a harder shove from the starboard side, pushing to port and almost off the highway. Our rig stumbled and shuddered, then started to tip. Lynn, who really is a calmer driver than I am, screamed.

"SLOW DOWN, LYNN!" I needn't have shouted. By then our blistering pace was about three miles per hour. It was only then that a couple of dogs raised their heads. Huh? What? Except poor Tiger. When the storm hit, he was frantic, which quickly turned to panic and on to outright sheer terror. It seemed like an eternity, but the storm passed.

The next day, we heard about the tornado in Sioux Falls. We unwittingly made it through unscathed, except for dear, dear Tiger who was shattered, stunned, and dazed. The happy big boy was never the same again in the motor home or even the car, no matter what the weather. At home, he was fine until an approaching storm. He would tell us hours ahead when there was trouble brewing over the horizon.

We spent a few days recovering from the storm at a beautiful KOA campground on the lower tip of the South Dakota Badlands. It was a tree-filled oasis surrounded by a starkly beautiful landscape that ran from wildly rugged, dry, hot, and desert-like on the north side to the treeless grasslands on the south. No major highways anywhere close by, and a surprising lack of airliner flight paths overhead made for a lovely time-travel to the past, with peaceful, quiet, sunny days. Night brought with it a sky absolutely awash and overflowing with stars, shiny cut crystals on black velvet. Spectacular sunrises and sunsets produced some of the loveliest colors I had ever seen, from an almost metallic gold to every shade of pink, purple, silver, and colors I cannot describe at all. Miles of hiking trails, abundant wildlife, and one of my favorite birds, the happy meadowlark, singing the summer song, completed the picture of our paradise. So it was from this little bit of heaven on Earth that we set off on the next leg of our adventure for Cody, Wyoming. But first it was on to the tiny town of Wall and the obligatory visit to Wall Drug where family fun is king! While there, we had one of those Old West photos taken with the dogs! As our troop entered the storefront, word must have spread quickly as a small crowd gathered to watch, not believing their eyes. With the picture done and a quick lunch, we were on our way.

Our excitement didn't last long. Ten miles west of Wall, the engine started to rev loudly, but we were slowing down! Pulling over, I checked for damage. A sad pool of rear end lubricant drained from the end of the axle shaft spilling onto yet another flat tire, and finally onto the ground. It told the frightful tale: Our rear axle had snapped.

Cell phone service was nonexistent. Our family vacation home on wheels was now a huge liability. For the moment, we were safe. Provisions were plentiful. The gas tank was full. That meant we had many, many hours to run the generator, which kept the air conditioner running, which was a good thing. At around noon, our outside thermometer read 93 degrees.

But with every semi-truck roaring by seemingly within inches of us, my fear heightened. Praying one of these guys wouldn't fall asleep at the wheel, we waited.

Just about the time buzzards started circling in the blazing afternoon sun, a kindly highway patrolman stopped by to check on us. Calling for a tow truck from Rapid City some fifty miles away, the officer bid us good luck, then peeled out after some scofflaw, we assumed.

Our relief faded over the hours as the promised help failed to show. Three-and-a-half hours later, the truck arrived. Yeah! At last! But the joy was cut short the closer it got. The driver and his helper looked like something akin to those cannibal woodsmen guys in the movie *Wrong Turn*.

They drew up in front of the coach and asked, "You the guy with the trouble?"

Shocked by their appearance and the fact that the tow truck looked like a Dumpster on wheels barely able to get out of its own way, I wanted to say, "No! We just stopped for a picnic and to risk death by a sleep-deprived semi driver. Thanks! Bye!" But all I could produce was a feeble squeak, "Ahhh, yes."

About then, Lynn, wearing a breezy summer outfit that included cool shorts, alighted down the steps, thankful for the rescue. Lynn is an attractive woman with great legs. Stopped cold by the hungry looks of our rescuers, she called out from a distance. "Thanks, fellas. Well, looks like you've got this handled, Pat," as she turned on her heel and dashed back in with the dogs, who were getting more inquisitive by the moment.

The driver, Denny, according to the name on the raggedy blue shirt, began to circle the motor home as if it were some kind of wild animal. Rubbing and scratching a dirty beard, he considered our problem and said, "Well, you ain't driving it. That's for sure. There's too much overhang in the rear. If we lift it up high enough in the front your rear end will drag."

"Hmmm, sounds painful," I injected, trying to brighten up the scene.

No response. After that, I stayed out of the way as they figured it out.

About an hour later, we were hooked up by the back end and ready to go. "You and the woman can get in the truck now." By this time, every dog was on full alert, protective, agitated, trying to peek out of every shade that Lynn had pulled down.

I edged back to the camper door, opening it just a crack.

"SHUT THE DOOR! YOU'RE EXCITING THE DOGS!" shouted Lynn.

"Me! Honey, it's time to go"

"I'll ride back here. Shut the door!"

I shot a nervous glance toward the truck. The men, leaning their backs against the wrecker, arms folded, were waiting for Lynn.

"Hey guys, she'll just ride back here."

"She can't."

"Hon, you can't...."

"I'll be all right."

"She'll be all right, fellas."

"State law says the wife can't ride back there."

"Hon, state law says..."

"I heard!"

This was like trying to peel a cat from a tree trunk.

"Lynn, we'll bring a couple of the dogs along. It will be fun!" My voice had a hollow, untrue ring, and she knew it.

"The woman will be right out, guys." I was still trying to be funny, but I should have quit while I was ahead.

A couple of minutes later, there she was in all her glory, wearing my best sweatshirt, a light jacket, baggy cargo pants, hiking boots, and a hat that would scare raccoons out of a garden. The guys looked at each other. Then it was the dogs' turn. Carla, the Rottweiler, and Tiger, the pit bull, bounded down the stairs, happy to be out and see who was causing all that commotion. Puffing up, straining on their leashes, they quickly placed themselves between the wrecker guys and us. The men straightened, finally reacting to something.

"Hope you don't think those dogs are going to ride in here. Not allowed. Might make a mess," they said.

Defeated again! Securing Carla and Tiger back in the motor

home, I told Lynn, it can't get any worse. It did.

Clambering up into the ancient truck, we were met by a foul stench, which Lynn would later recall as a days-old dead body. *More like rotten food*, was my thought.

One of them said, "Your wife can ride in the sleeper." She shot a look that burned right through me. Lynn refused to talk about her ride back there afterward, and I never brought it up again. She did, however, burn the clothes she was wearing during that ride at the next campsite, including my favorite old sweatshirt.

It took about two-and-a-half painful, sweaty hours to make the trip to Rapid City. Other than smelling like an odd combination of old motor oil, diesel fuel, moldy food, and death, we made it in fine fettle. We were alive and uneaten! The wrecker guys set us down in kind of an industrial area at Godfrey's Heavy Truck and Brake Repair. Denny had me sign a work order, then with a grunt, handed us a copy, and the two raced out of the lot down to the local watering hole, I imagined.

I shall always miss the sparkling conversations and intellectual stimulation we shared that July day. We had the pleasure of being towed numerous times with that motor home, as the rig fell apart faster than we could repair it. In every other instance, we found the wrecker operators professional, clean, and pleasant. Things vastly improved for us at Godfrey's where we spent most of the rest of our vacation. The employees were nothing less than the milk of human kindness. They set about blocking and leveling the motor home, in such a way so they could make the repairs, and we could stay in it until the job was completed. They even hooked up the water and electricity. The office staff offered to do our laundry.

The owner lent us an old truck to visit the Black Hills, see Deadwood, and snoop around Rapid City. He even gave us the keys to the lot so we could come and go as we pleased at night.

Waiting for hard-to-come-by parts caused us to stay a lot longer than we had hoped. But the experience helped us realize that good old-fashioned American hospitality was still alive and well, and the treatment we received made our stay comfortable and pleasant, except for the final bill, which was almost $3,000.

In the end, there was no Cody, Wyoming, or Yellowstone Park on this trip. But we packed in enough adventures, stories, and tales that we could share many times over the years. Not fun then, but I wouldn't trade them for anything. Lynn's thoughts may differ just a tad.

⁓

Not all of our out-of-town excursions involved the motor home. In our minivan, we took a weekend jaunt to visit Lynn's parents in Chicago traveling with Ruby, Carla, Tiger, and Hilde. (Venus stayed with friends.)

It was close to midnight on a Friday as we pulled up to a Super 8 in Janesville, Wisconsin. I dashed in to the lobby.

"Good evening, sir," whispered the young woman behind the desk. While filling out the registration forms, I offhandedly mentioned we had pets.

"Dogs, sir?"

"Ahh, yes," now my voice was barely audible.

Receiving our room assignment, I attempted to beat a hasty retreat to the van. Just a couple of feet from the front door and freedom, I was busted!

"Sir," the young woman asked, "what kind of dogs are they? How many?" I imagine she was hoping to hear poodle, Pomeranian, or sheltie.

Strolling back to the desk, I put on a happy, confident face. "Oh,

I'm sorry," I said in bright, elevated tones. "Two pit bulls and two Rottweilers."

Her face froze with unblinking eyes. She seemed to pale more by the moment. I waited with a serene smile, glasses riding low down on my nose. I suppose I looked like an English professor expecting a brilliant answer from a student. But for a while, there was nothing.

At last, her eyes started to blink rapidly, a sure sign of stress! "Ahhh...ummm, what time do you plan on checking out, sir?" I got her drift: Please leave before my boss sees what I've done.

"Around sunrise, ma'am. We need an early start," I answered. And so we did.

A final note on our travels. Readers most likely are left wondering, "Why would anyone want to travel in a motor home or with that many dogs?" I'll admit, our first rig was a money pit, causing at times much angst, bickering, battling, brawling, and looking for roadside divorce lawyer signs.

Our current vacation home on wheels has been dead stone reliable and worry free. It's now an absolute joy to see America, especially with the dogs! The people we've met along the way come from every point of the spectrum. Each has a fascinating story if you listen.

CHAPTER EIGHT

Owning a Pit Bull Ain't Easy

Before adding pit bulls to the family mix, Lynn and I had Rottweilers for many years. We found them to be stable, fun loving, sweet, smart, and sturdy. In early training, we also found them to be willful and stubborn on occasion. They often tested us during their informative period. But once they understood and respected us as the alphas, we had great dogs for life. Part of that training was to keep the dog socialized, always exposing it to places, people, street sounds, and other dogs.

Over the years, Lynn and I have taken our share of bumps walking the Rottweilers in public. Certainly, a lot of people appreciated the manners they displayed and their stately, yet friendly, demeanor. Then there were those, although small in numbers, who weren't so pleased to see us. They were quite vocal with their opinions about the type of people who owned such dogs.

When we brought a pit bull into the family fold, we expected some additional grief. What we received was more dirty looks and rude comments, in spite of our dogs being on leashes and well behaved!

A favorite summer weekend getaway of ours was the city of Duluth. Sitting on Lake Superior about two-and-a-half hours north of Minneapolis/St. Paul, the city perches on steep hills overlooking the largest freshwater lake in the world. It is a city in transition, from serious decline in the 1970s to a town reinventing itself as a lovely tourist destination with nice shops, restaurants, and hotels on the once notorious waterfront. The shoreline is rocky, craggy, and beautiful. It reminded me very much of the seacoast of Maine sans the salt air. Lake Superior was capable of violent storms that would do the Atlantic proud. While in Duluth one glorious late spring day, Lynn and I were enjoying a stroll on the boardwalk that separated the city from the lake. Starting at Canal Park, running along the water for five miles, it's a great place for dog walking. That is unless you're walking pit bulls and Rottweilers. Whenever we met a large group of people, or those with dogs, Lynn and I would always step aside to let them pass. No matter how many times we've made way for others, many people cast a wary eye in our direction, stepping off the walk opposite us. We have received many hateful, angry looks from others.

The real topper in experiencing hate and fear in Duluth came one afternoon just as we were heading back to the car. Three couples with children in tow were ahead of us. Clipping along at a faster pace, we were just about to pass them when one of the mothers glanced back. A blood-curdling scream assaulted our ears. We pulled up short, wondering what had happened. Others on the busy walkway, including the rest of her party, stopped to see what the commotion was about. The mother launched into a tirade as she and the others grabbed the children.

The mom screeched, "What are you doing here with those ugly, horrible dogs! They aren't allowed here!" (This was not true.) She turned her attention to the kids, preschool- and elementary school-aged. By this time she was practically hissing. "Those are dogs of war. They kill people, and they love the taste of blood, especially children's blood!" Holy crap! The woman was not only attacking us, but also doing a fine job of traumatizing the kids! The dogs, to their credit, were standing around wondering, "What's going on?"

Panzer mom continued, "People who own dogs like that are evil and mean. They hurt people and just like to make them afraid. That's why they have those kinds of dogs!"

Lynn couldn't stand another utterance. She launched a defensive counterattack. Her words not only fell on deaf ears, but also whipped up the rest of the mom's group into a kind of mob mentality. Now all of them were jeering us with a generous sprinkling of profanity.

A couple of walkers passing by the scene apparently thought our dogs must have caused a problem and joined in the fray. Trying to reason with these people was pointless. We took a shortcut back to the car, their shouts ringing in our ears. Mentally bloodied, we left town. This day belonged to the victors.

We understood that when taking our dogs out amongst the populous, they look imposing, which was why we went to great lengths to try and not make people feel uncomfortable. I guess just taking the dogs out was bad enough. There were bright spots that day, some small victories of our own. People came up wanting to pet the dogs and ask questions. There were even some who changed their minds, or at the very least started thinking, seeing beyond the hype and urban legends.

Duluth is not a hotbed of prejudice. Back home in the metro area, numerous communities held weekly summer events that celebrated one thing or another with a carnival atmosphere. A couple of them Lynn and I attended regularly to meet friends, to socialize, and to savor a beautiful Minnesota summer evening.

It's funny how you sometimes run into the same person time and time again. If the person happened to be a member of the opposite gender, it could be a good thing. That's how I met Lynn. We kept bumping into each other at collector car shows. I found out she liked dogs, old cars, old houses, and old guys. Hey, worked for me! Other times running into the same person isn't so much fun, especially if they are mean-spirited jerks. One fellow was particularly troublesome. Stocky, graying hair pulled into a ponytail, a grubby manner of dress, he had an attitude on one shoulder and a chip on the other. This guy hated our pack. Not just pitties. Not just Rotties. He hated both! So it didn't matter what combination of kids we had along. This guy would follow behind us making the usual comments in an impressive vocal range. When that didn't affect us or cause Lynn and me to leave, this porky curmudgeon decided to change his rhetoric to something a bit more colorful. "Those dogs should be run through a meat grinder," which in short order turned into, "If I get my hands on those dogs, I'll shoot 'em and put them through the meat grinder myself."

For two summers, this guy kept bumping into us at various functions. Toward the end of the second summer, Mr. Sunshine raised the stakes once again, suggesting that the owners of the dogs should be shot and run through that meat grinder as well. Now, he was more than a pesky nuisance. I talked with a friend who was a captain in the sheriff's department. The captain had a "come to Jesus" meeting with the jolly old soul. Since then, we've had nary a spot of real trouble with the guy.

A miraculous thing did occur during those summer outings. More and more people saw our tribe. They noted the mannerly dispositions of our kids. A number of them noted, too, that dreadful man harassing us. They were actually supportive of us. The fan base of Carla, Tiger, Venus, and Ruby grew impressively. On the rare evenings when Lynn and I went alone, people were worried. "Where is so and so and so and so? Why did you come without them? Are they okay?" It seemed they were more interested in seeing the dogs than seeing us, wanting to pet and hug the lovable lugs. Things were looking up!

But another incident marred an otherwise pleasant night that summer. A young woman rushed out of a thick crowd, threw herself onto the ground in front of Carla, grabbing the surprised dog by the cheeks and kissing her between the eyes. Carla barked a mighty bark in the woman's face as they both leapt back. The woman shrieked, "How can you have such a dangerous dog in public?!" as her friends rallied around her, leading the poor shaken girl away. Despite happenings like that from time to time, we periodically started to think things truly were getting better. But still, there were days that left us shaken and scratching our heads. This time, it was practically in our very own backyard.

It was an unusually warm Thanksgiving Day in 2007. Around 11:00 a.m., Lynn and I decided to take a quiet, pleasant walk in the park about a block away from the house. Snow had not yet arrived in our little town so the trek would be easy. We planned to take the crew, one pair at a time. Carla and Ruby were hooked up first and rearing to go! Not expecting anyone at the park, we were mildly surprised to see a father and young son playing on the tunnels and slides as we passed by on our way to the ball fields. They were far away enough as we passed by that I would not have recognized them in a line-up if my life depended upon it.

Then the father started yelling that we should get the hell out of the park, that we had vicious, dangerous dogs, that he was a lawyer, and that he could make real trouble for us. Then he turned his focus on me, "You must have a short one! What's the matter? Can't please your wife, so ya have to compensate with those bastards?"

Lynn asked him to leave us alone, but he zeroed in on her. The rotten excuse for a human hurled a few more insults at Lynn, so vulgar, I can't and won't include them here. I turned to confront him.

"Pat! Don't you dare go over there!" Lynn was firm. "If he calls the police on you, he'll probably say the dogs chased him."

We usually carried along newspaper articles on Ruby to help allay fears people may have. But they have to be willing to listen. I was sure this man wasn't a listener.

Unbelievably, Lynn walked over to him. I was furious, but stayed put. Perfectly calm, she tried to show him the newspapers. Knocking them out of her hands, he shouted, "Get out of here!" On her way back to Carla, Ruby, and me, he kept up the barrage. But this time his young son had joined in, hands on hips, an angry expression across his face, shouting unintelligible comments.

We did finish the walk, but it was a pall cast over Thanksgiving that year.

Early the next week, I called J.P. Barone, an assistant state attorney general for Minnesota. J.P., having done community theater with Ruby, knew her behavior well and was a fan of hers. I told him the story of the colorful lawyer in the park. Mr. Barone asked Lynn and me to get his name and law firm if possible. "He should be investigated for his abhorrent behavior while representing himself as an attorney." Unfortunately, we had never seen this man before, so we were dead in the water. But it was nice to know Ruby had friends in high places who could vouch for her.

I certainly understand parents wanting to protect their families from vicious dogs. I understand, too, that many cities feel they have a pit bull problem. We all have the right to enjoy our yards, ride a bike, or go for a walk, or go to the park unmolested and unafraid. The dogs were not the problem. The real problem is the human element. We were the problem, we could be the solution. But it won't be easy.

Family Time

SADIE AND RUBY RELAX

SADIE SURROUNDED BY DOGS, CHRISTMAS 2010.
L TO R VENUS, MOLLY, RUBY, TIGER, CARLA

Ruby

LOOKIN' SPORTY!

"CHEAPER BY THE DOZEN"

A SENIOR OPENS UP TO
THE "RUBSTER".

Ruby

A SENIOR REMEMBERS...
A KID AGAIN.

RUBY KISSES ARE BEST!

RUBY AND MOLLY
ENJOY THE SUN

ON THE ROAD WITH RUBY

Ruby's Travels

I'VE...

HAD
ADVENTURES
IN THE DESERT.

CHECKED OUT "THE CORN
PALACE". ZZZ

...BEEN FORCED TO RIDE THIS
STUPID THING!

VISITED WALL DRUG

Ruby's Travels

I'VE...

RIDDEN IN A COVERED WAGON ACROSS THE PRAIRIE.

TAKEN NAPS WITH MY SISTER.

BEEN A TIME TRAVELER.

California

CALIFORNIA BOUND!

AM I CUTE OR WHAT?

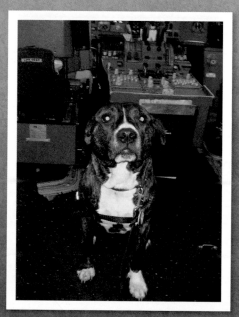

"THIS IS NOT MY JOB!"

THE FLIGHT CREW
LOVED RUBY

RUBY LOVES BONNIE HUNT!

Chicago

I HATE WAITING IN AIRPORTS

LET'S CHECK IN!

OH! OH! PAPARAZZI!

NOW, FOR A GREAT MEAL

I FEEL SO REGAL!!!

IT'S THIS DOG'S LIFE

Miami

I LOVE MY JOB!

ENOUGH ABOUT MY
DOUBLE CHIN!

I LOVE YOU TOO DOC...

MIAMI NICE

On a fall Saturday afternoon in 2008, Lynn, Ruby, and I were out for a walk around Como Lake in St. Paul. As a young man approached us head on, we noted that he had a cute white-and-brown pit bull puppy, a friendly little guy. Without thinking, I reached down to pet him. The young man started to slap and kick the dog!

"What the hell are you doing?" I bellowed.

He returned fire, "I don't want a nice dog."

I could only imagine the life ahead of that innocent puppy. I wanted to follow him and steal the dog. We cried for that helpless little life. And we were angry! Bad owners are the bane of every responsible, caring, loving pet parent. Then there were the politicians who put all pit bull owners in the same pot. "We don't want the kind of people who own pit bulls in our town," commented the mayor of a Colorado city.

I'd like to eliminate the bad owners, too, and while there seems to be plenty of them, the far majority of pit bulls are owned by good, solid pet parents. Their dogs live quiet, happy lives, doing no harm, and in fact give to the community as therapy, search and rescue, or law enforcement dogs. That's right—a growing number of law enforcement agencies have discovered an unsurpassed work ethic in the pit bull for drug and explosives detection. They are tireless in the job and great with the public. At last report, the Washington state patrol has six or seven on board.

The Drug Enforcement Administration also uses them. One, named Popsicle, saved from a locked refrigerator during a drug raid, went on to make the biggest drug bust ever. Cook County Sheriff's Department in Chicago hired a pit bull. They jokingly said the biggest problem they had was that "It's too friendly with people." A problem all agencies face is public perception.

Since Ruby was tested and certified as a service dog, the public perception has changed considerably, at least toward her. When she's wearing the service dog cape, people are fascinated, shocked, and disbelieving. They ask questions, making sure what they are seeing is real. Others seem to have an epiphany: "So pit bulls can be good dogs! That's not what you read in the papers or see on TV. What is the truth?" Then, for what seems to be the millionth time, I begin, "There was this puppy left to die..."

CHAPTER NINE

Ruby, Accolades, and the Media

From the beginning, I had plans for Ruby to become a therapy dog. Also, the media should cover it—a starving rescue dog that just happens to be a pit bull contributing to the community. The story could encourage others to adopt a shelter dog and do something wonderfully positive for others...for themselves. I had been accused of being a relentless, unrepentant publicity hound wanting glory heaped upon myself. In part, that was true, at least for our theater company. But I had my day in the sun. It was all about Ruby now, all about adoption, all about the great things you can achieve with your once homeless little dog. I've often said Ruby was a great dog, but there are millions of great dogs out there including legions of pitties owned by loving, caring, responsible owners. In fact, there are lots of pit bulls better than Ruby. Thankfully she can't read...yet!

Before her stage play, a couple of short stories appeared in small local papers when she received her TDI certification in November 2005. Major media refused to take note. But with *Cheaper by the Dozen* in September 2006, people began to talk. One evening a reporter from the Minneapolis *Star Tribune* was in the audience. He was there to interview Jack Rhodes, but the little girl with the small dog touched his heart. After the performance, as the cast was slapping each other on the back telling themselves how wonderful they were, the reporter stopped by to say he couldn't talk now, but please call in a couple of days. He wanted to do a story about Ruby.

Within a week, he and a photographer visited Ruby at the Croixdale Residence while she worked her quiet charm on the seniors. The article quickly followed with the lead-in "Golden Agers Welcome Ruby, the Pit Bull with a Heart of Gold." It was a nice, positive piece. It was soon followed by a front-page story in an East Metro paper with a great color photo of the little girl, Katie, tenderly holding Ruby's face. The headline read, "Ruby, Newest Lakeshore Player—Rescue Dog, a Star in *Cheaper by the Dozen*." Close on the heels of that article, the same reporter, Mike Morgan, ran a follow-up story under the title "Blame the Deed, Not the Breed." Mike described Ruby in glowing terms. "Fabulous dog…Calmest dog I've ever seen…cuddly." Far more than that, he addressed the reputation of her breed. Mike did his research well. In his conclusion, he asked, what's wrong with this picture? On the one hand you have Ruby, on the other hand you have hyped-up media images of pit bull–type dogs that maim or kill. He summed it up quite well. "It's the owners that are the problem."

Whew! It had been a fun year for Ruby. It had also been a busy one, with visiting two senior residences a week, auditioning for and performing in the play, and fulfilling family obligations. There had been barely enough time to be just a dog…lazy and silly. Thankfully we were approaching the holidays with Thanksgiving less than a month away. Ruby could use some down time about now. But fate often has a completely different sense of timing.

"What's this, hon?" I asked Lynn as I looked through the mail one Saturday morning in early November 2006.

"No clue," she answered.

It was from the Minnesota Veterinary Medical Association.

Opening it I read, "Ruby has been nominated for induction into the Minnesota Veterinary Medical Association Animal Hall of Fame. Please fill out this form and return it immediately." Huh?! We checked out the association on the web. It seemed legit. So off went the form...soon forgotten. That was, until December 14 when another envelope arrived.

"I am contacting you to congratulate you and your dog. Ruby is the recipient of the MVMA Animal Hall of Fame Companion Award. The ceremony will take place at noon on Saturday, February 3, 2007, at the Hilton Hotel in Minneapolis." I was stunned. How great was this for rescue dogs, for pit bulls, for Ruby! But how, why did it happen? I soon found out that two veterinarians, Dr. Yoho and Dr. Waters, from Ruby's Stillwater Clinic had been impressed by her work in the community, her behavior, and her deep goodness. The holidays whizzed past. I was excited, even a bit nervous. If she was jittery, Ruby didn't show it, greeting each day with the usual head shake, body shake, a scratch or two at an ear followed by a brief hygiene session, potty, breakfast, then nap till I took her to work with me at noon.

The media attention picked up again. But not to the degree I thought it would. There were a couple of small newspaper articles, but nothing from television...until just a few days before the ceremony. Rob Olsen from Fox 9 News visited the radio station where Ruby and I worked and filmed an absolutely terrific piece. Apparently this story had quite a following. People were recognizing Ruby on the street. "Excuse me, is (pause) that the dog on TV?" became fairly common.

On the morning of the day Ruby was to receive her award, we were scheduled to appear on the local CBS affiliate with Dr. Hunter, the president of MVMA. Things didn't go so smoothly this time. The male host whose name I have thankfully forgotten and am equally thankful he's no longer there was ill-prepared for the interview. He asked dumb questions, made stupid comments, and was also disrespectful to Dr. Hunter. His rapport with Ruby was abysmal. She gave him a look of great disdain as he continued to call her "boy" and poke at her in quick thrusts as if she had fleas. By the time he asked, "Why do these dogs have such a bad reputation?" I had had it! I lost any media savvy I possessed. Putting my hand on his shoulder, my answer was simple, "Because of bad owners and you in the media." Oh, I could have kicked myself!

After, in the green room, he was not a happy man, becoming more pompous and very angry. We beat a hasty retreat to the Hilton. Not long after our appearance, I heard the poor guy lost his job (nothing to do with us!). To be fair, in November 2008, the same affiliate did a great story by a smart reporter (Liz Collin) who knew what she was doing.

The event itself was great fun, humbling, and just a little surreal. Several hundred veterinarians were in attendance including Dr. Fitzgerald from *Animal Planet*. Did we really deserve all this fuss? Though admittedly, there were other dogs receiving awards, Ruby was content to think it was all about her. Barely glancing up as their achievements were read, still impeccably mannered, Ruby was becoming a diva.

The play and the hall of fame award were preparatory steps for what the future held, but in the meantime, there was work to be done: regular visits to senior residences, nursing homes, hospice patients, and, as the local celebrity dog, helping host a number of animal rescue fundraisers. It was at one of these events that I was reminded of the importance that kids (along with adults) must learn to control their dogs. My attention was focused on a woman who had questions about therapy dogs, qualifications, and Ruby (who was lying at my feet). My peripheral vision caught a white streak off to the left. I turned just in time to see a Jack Russell terrier grab Ruby's face. A twelve-year-old girl clumsily chased after the dog to catch up and grab the leash. But the damage had been done. Ruby leapt back as I kicked the offending dog, breaking its grip. The girl, not saying a word to me, grabbed the leash and pleaded with the dog to follow. I was furious! I wanted to follow her to have a talk with her parents. But Ruby was bleeding from puncture wounds above and below her eye.

Inspection showed her eye to be okay, thank God! The girl and the dog? Disappeared. This was the third time Ruby had been bitten in a sneak attack. But it was the first time blood had been drawn. In all three attacks, she had not attempted a defensive counterattack. Had she, and the other dog been injured, the whole thing would have been blamed on the pit bull.

The previous year, 2007, had been a good one for Ruby: an award, some fun in the sun, camping, and swimming. Ruby was certainly on the small side, but at fifty-four pounds, she was thickly muscled, rock-like in the water. Lynn had decided to get a couple of life jackets for the pitties. What a difference! While Tiger enjoyed the simple pleasure of swimming back and forth, Ruby became a shark, with water lilies as her favorite victims.

There was her therapy work and personal appearances, and on December 14, 2007, Ruby received an achievement award for her work in the community. It was from the Animal Farm Foundation out of New York! Their mission was to restore the image of the original America's Hero Dog, the pit bull. We weren't aware that we were even on the foundation's radar! Topping all that off, there was talk of a new pack member coming from China! Life was good. But someone over the horizon wanted to kill Ruby or, at the very least, banish her and all those like her from the state.

It was early December 2007; Lynn was about to leave for China to pick up Sadie. Again, a reporter from the Minneapolis *Star Tribune* and a good acquaintance of Jack Rhodes decided to do a major article on Ruby. Recently, she had done a piece on Jack. That theme was what people who work in the criminal justice system do for relaxation and fun. Motorcycles and plays were his thing. By now, Jack and I had done several shows together. Apparently he spent enough time talking about his fellow four-legged actor that the reporter, Pat Phiffer, had her curiosity piqued. So it was that the *Star Tribune* came out to the Croixdale Residence once more. But this time things would be different. They were prepared to do a major story. Ms. Phiffer, a still photographer, and a video photographer spent a lot of time with Ruby. It was obvious they cared about the story they were working on. Interestingly, Pat Phiffer's brother ran a dog training school and didn't allow pitties to take classes (which to my way of thinking is a flawed policy; how are responsible pit bull owners going to train and socialize their dogs in a structured setting?). During the time they spent there, the newspaper crew was respectful of the seniors, the location, and Ruby. As she was leaving, Ms. Phiffer said, "Pat, you know, I'm going to take a lot of heat on this. It goes against public perception."

On December 19, Lynn left for China with eighteen other couples to meet their new family members. Lynn received Sadie on Christmas Eve. At 23 months old, she would change our lives. But we had no idea how Sadie's and Ruby's lives would intersect with such impact.

On Saturday, December 29, 2007, the Ruby article hit the newsstands. I was blown away! Located on the front page of the second section, the piece went on for two pages with colored pictures. (I was told later that it was the most read story in the paper that day.) The online video that went with the piece was viewed in China by Lynn and the other families. Technology...how cool! This was a major coup for us. Now people were really starting to take notice. But there was more to come. Much more!

The newspaper coverage would help in a very public battle led by a politician to ban five breeds of dogs in the state, including pit bulls and Rottweilers. If his proposed law passed, the targeted breeds would be seized and destroyed if they weren't removed from the state. Those harboring such dogs would face prison time and fines. It didn't matter the dog's credentials. If your dog was on the hit list, it was gone. So there you have it—Ruby and I were possibly legislated to criminals on the lam. It was unfair to all responsible owners and their family members.

The push for breed banning came after several tragic pit bull attacks in the Twin Cities metro area including the frightful, tragic death of a young boy in Minneapolis by a "family" pit bull as reported by the media. It was no family pet. The killer was an unsocialized, unneutered male tethered by a very short chain to a pole in the basement, and he had a history of terrorizing people. There was a female pit bull with puppies nearby. When the boy and his friends went downstairs to visit the puppies, the boy got too close to the male and was killed. This was not a family dog. It was a dog in residence. The father of the victim just happened to have a loaded pistol nearby and shot the dog. As I understand it, the female dog was not involved in the attack. I won't hazard a guess as to what was going on in that house, but I have a pretty fair idea.

Sometime before his trial, the father tried to contact me through the newspaper and radio station. I never returned his calls. I assumed he wanted help in his defense. These kinds of owners drive me crazy! Yes, it was a bad dog, but why? Had some other loving, kind person who understood the responsibilities of training and socialization had this dog, the resultant dog most likely might have been a far different soul.

On the other hand, a number of legislators took note of the Minneapolis *Star Tribune* article. They started asking questions, coming to the same conclusion as the reporter in an earlier article. Here we have Ruby gathering awards for her work in the community. Over there you have the same breed that's taken a child's life. What's going on here? By the end of the session, cooler, brighter heads prevailed. Laws that targeted the bad owners rather than the breed of dog were passed. The new laws still aren't strong enough, in my opinion, but then nobody's made me king. At least they are a step in the right direction. I could not say the Ruby publicity swayed the lawmakers singlehandedly, but it sure didn't hurt! But there were a lot of terrific people working tirelessly behind the scenes with the lawmakers.

When you tell lawmakers and critics that your pit bull "Fluffy" loves kids and wouldn't hurt a flea, they are unmoved, unbelieving. More likely they're thinking, "Yeah, right!" When the media covers a pittie with certified credentials and quantified results of their work, the skeptics are caught off guard and flat-footed. There are those, however, who will think it a cheap trick, the media manipulated.

It's amazing how some stories go on for a long time. The December 2007 Minneapolis *Star Tribune* story was picked up by the Associated Press and spread quickly throughout the United States then on to Europe. The real culmination of the article's effect came one day about two months after it initially ran in the *Star Tribune*. Ruby was busy with visiting rounds at Croixdale Residence when Mary Jo Duclow, the activities director, handed me a page written in French from a Fribourg, Switzerland, newspaper dated February 4, 2008. The daughter of a Croixdale resident lived in Fribourg and in her note, she said, "As I was reading the paper last evening, I came across this story. Couldn't believe my eyes, mother lives at Croixdale!" Apparently, it caused quite a stir as pit bulls were not highly regarded on the other side of the pond either. The attention Ruby was garnering began to make a real difference in the way people looked at pit bulls. But it wasn't enough.

Spring of 2008 brought a call from Karen Delise, the author of a number of books who was writing an article for the e-newsletter of the mayor's Alliance for New York City Animals. She wanted to know if Ruby could be one of the featured dogs in the piece. The story ran that August. I started to suspect that Ruby was maintaining an apartment in New York.

Yes, Ruby has accomplished much, but if you don't keep it up, people soon forget. With that in mind, Ruby and I set about attacking the national media. A Ruby packet was developed, which contained newspaper articles, a DVD, and pictures, and listed her accomplishments and accolades. Fox News Network, CNN, *Good Morning America*, *The Today Show*, and *The Early Show* were all approached. Only Fox News replied. "Seems like you have a nice accomplished dog. Keep up the good work." No matter, it's just part of the territory. Many years of fundraising for a non-profit taught me about rejection. I didn't have to like it. I'd just try to find another way to sell the media Ruby's story, but in a good-humored soft sell sort of way. It could be a fine line though, and if you make enemies in the media, stick a fork in you because you're done.

A local, small-town weekly newspaper did the first-ever Ruby story. It was a decent piece, with a cute picture. Then a new editor took over just as Ruby's fame grew. He saw no reason to do a hometown angle on Ruby's induction into the Animal Hall of Fame. It seemed he wanted to be an enemy, and I had no clue as to why. He'd just sit back in his chair, smile, and reject any and all story ideas. I didn't know who he was or why he copped this attitude. Ruby flew to Hollywood. "Not newsworthy." Ruby's picture to appear on Milk-Bone boxes around the world. "Not interested." I gave up on Mr. Editor and his odd demeanor, but will admit, he bothers me a little when I think of him.

Media coverage really caught hold during Ruby's Milk-Bone campaign. Television, newspapers, and radio all had the "Ruby bug" to one degree or another. Television stations did in-studio interviews and at-home stories. Newspaper coverage kept tabs on Ruby's campaign trail.

In the end, the media has been very kind to Ruby. It took a while to get their attention, but once they discovered her, they stuck by her. National media has been a tougher nut to crack. We're working on it, though. Ruby's story isn't over, not by a long shot.

CHAPTER TEN

And Baby Makes Nine!

"You're adopting a what!? Are you sure? I mean, at your age...it's...well, what about the dogs? You're going to have to get rid of some!" Our friend never did hold back her opinions.

The October 2007 announcement of our soon-to-arrive daughter from China proved to be no barrier to her giving us both barrels. Lynn and I had actually started the paperwork a couple of years before. We started to tell those closest to us that we planned to adopt, but before we could finish they'd interrupt with, "What kind? Do you truly need another dog?" After hearing the rest of our story, the reaction was somewhat more subdued: "Really? Gee. *Really?*" In the interim some friends either forgot about our plans, thinking them far into the future, or more likely thought we would abandon our intentions altogether, seeing the light at our age.

The announcement that Lynn would be leaving for China within a few months to pick up two-year-old Sadie Marie sent shock waves through our network of friends, though nothing so overt as little miss sunshine's warm, fuzzy concern about our age and the dogs. There was a definite cooling from those we expected it least...just small things they said, questions asked and a distinct lack of enthusiasm for the blessed event unfolding. But no doubt about it, their concern was the same as our razor-tongued friend. We in turn were saddened.

In truth, Lynn had fears. "What if Sadie was terrified of the dogs?" "What if the dogs didn't like Sadie?" "A new member, forced into the pack, I just don't know." From my perspective, the main concern was if Sadie had allergies. Either way, getting rid of the furry side of the family was out of the question.

Getting the pack to accept her was a non-issue for me, having done it with my older daughter Tracy many years before. My practice had been then, as it was now, the same. There would be no screeching and kicking at the dog(s) to get away when first bringing home the baby. This was vital. You're sure to foster resentment if you do! We would not shove the baby in their faces. This was just as important. We would not discourage gentle curiosity, but make them feel part of something special and wonderful, and this would garner positive results. Giving them a job to help put the little one to bed or feed baby was great. A slow, commonsense approach to physically introducing the new child and the pack to each other was best. All the time and effort we put into blending the family paid big dividends and was worth every minute. But all of that was a couple of months ahead of us.

For the moment, we had to deal with others' (including some family members') anxiety. There were those who felt we were committing something tantamount to child abuse by throwing an innocent toddler into a pack of dogs with unpredictable results. "Gee! Sure appreciate the kind words. We're so glad you have faith that we might kinda know what we are doing!" Admittedly, that negative remark came from outside our circle of friends. They also were not dog people. They really didn't know us, know our furry kids, and certainly didn't know Sadie. None of us knew Sadie yet. If we had, any worries would have turned to dust.

On January 5, 2008, Lynn's plane touched down at the Minneapolis Airport. The little dynamo named Sadie from Wuxi, China, was about to be unleashed upon North America. Everybody, and I mean everybody, was soon whistling a different tune.

A startlingly beautiful child, she was at first shy with a deer-in-the-headlights look when friends and family greeted or rather overwhelmed her at the airport. One couple had even brought their dog...ours waited at home. Sadie had just spent two weeks getting used to Lynn in China, forming a bond with her. Now it was another big change. Everything in the world that she knew was now gone. Even the comfort of her language (Mandarin) had vanished. Lynn and I tried to learn some reassuring phrases that were probably bungled in the translation. But at least we attempted some form of communication. With all the tumult at the terminal, it was hard to tell if they worked. After dinner out with the well wishers, shouts of congratulations, good luck, and good-byes faded into the night, the three of us were alone. Lynn was tired, zapped, exhausted, and running on empty. Sadie seemed none the worse for wear having slept on the plane. I was astonished when Lynn mentioned that the little one hadn't cried on the flight. "What little kid doesn't cry on a plane? Is she okay?" Sadie was fine. It was an early indicator of how tough and resilient she was to be. For now, there was one more task at hand.

Entering our house seemed like a strangely solemn moment. This was to be the start of Sadie's new life, where so many memories, imprints, life's lessons, and family events would mold her into the person she would become. Sadie's furry siblings were also oddly sedate as we arrived home. I would call it a soft curiosity. Under controlled conditions, one by one they entered the meet-and-greet room gently sniffing this newcomer.

Hilde and Venus showed only a passing interest and moved on.

If young Molly could talk, it would have gone something like the following: "Okay, okay, she's nice. Now pet me. Hey! Got treats?" Tiger wiggled happily as best he could, gave her a gentle snort, and curled up close by, ready for a nap. Ruby had a joyful attitude of let me see... let me see! I'll be careful! As with Tiger, Ruby wanted to stay, but like the others she was ushered out. Sadie's reaction to the dogs was sort of anticlimactic. There was no reaction. She eyed each one with care, studying them. She didn't try to reach out or touch them that night. Sadie showed no fear at all! It looked as if she was trying to figure out what kind of life form they were. Most certainly she had never seen dogs at the orphanage.

There was one more family member standing patiently by the baby gate. Carla swept into the room as if she knew this was to be the role in life she had been born for — nanny to Sadie! Carla tenderly sniffed her from head to toe. Carla's hind end with that stub of a tail practically fell off from all that high-speed vibrating. It was instant love. From that minute on, Carla became Sadie's protector, her shadow. Carla was the first one to greet her in the morning, the last one to tuck her in at night, and the one who licked the tears from her cheeks. During the first few weeks while Sadie was adjusting to the time change, Carla checked on her several times a night, quietly standing by the gate whenever she fussed a bit. Ruby liked Sadie well enough, enjoyed snuggling with her, but it was Carla who relished her new job.

So, the expected carnage never happened as life around our house took on a new, busier dimension. It was a while before something resembling a rhythm settled in. It had been a long time since I had had a two-year-old in the house. I was reminded frequently that they are a lot more work than five well-trained dogs. At last, once a system had been established, things went smoothly. Meal times were always a favorite of the "kids." Tidbits falling from Sadie's highchair seemed to be in ample supply. You never saw dogs so attentive to a child. One day we noticed that she was dropping food down to the dogs for entertainment. Dogs were now banished from the dining room.

In the following weeks and months as a new huge world opened to Sadie, her language skills improved at a dramatic pace. The power-packed little kid rose to every challenge without fear. She became a social butterfly, unafraid to communicate with anyone. With the dogs, Sadie became alpha toddler, barking out orders. No! Sit! Stay! Alpha yes, but she felt warmly comfortable around them. She loved their company, showing them deep tenderness.

The relationship was smooth except for a brief spot at about her three-and-a-half-year mark. During a quiet evening as we were gathered in the den, Sadie decided it might be fun to bite Ruby's tail! Ruby leapt straight up, whipped around, and porpoised Sadie in the face with her nose as if to say, "Stop it!" Shortly after, one more incident occurred. While riding in the car, Molly loved to lean against the kiddie car seat, head draped onto Sadie's lap. We were on our way home from some function, and it was far later than we cared to be out and about. Suddenly a loud pained yip startled Lynn and me, while Molly took off to the far back of the car. Sadie admitted to biting poor Molly's ear. Luckily, it was the last biting episode. Sadie had learned both times that she earned Mom and Dad's extreme displeasure plus numerous privileges and goodies taken away. These were not stuffed animals. Disrespect toward or pain inflicted upon another living thing would not be tolerated. That lesson was for her own safety as well as a perfect example of why children should not be left alone with pets. We knew Sadie was not a mean or sadistic child. Her actions were out of character. It was simply childhood curiosity, a kid acting goofy. But the behavior had to be nipped in the bud.

Wherever Sadie went, people just wanted to see her and to be near the beautiful, outgoing child who was so relaxed in public. The concerned friends who became standoffish when the adoption was really close at hand had changed their opinions. "Aww, look at how good she is with dogs!" Or, "It's amazing to see how respectfully the dogs treat her!" They were now fully smitten over the intelligent, happy little dynamo with the incredible life force willing to try anything new, eat anything different, and greet anyone with that killer smile.

From her very first days in America, Sadie attended dog-training classes. She was a fast learner; only her pint size prevented her from training a dog on her own. The problem was that Sadie was so relaxed and comfortable around dogs, she would want to go up to any strange animal and start petting or hugging. This could be bad. Oddly, it was hard for her to learn to ask first, although it got better. I suppose, like most kids, if it's something for their own best interest, it's a lesson quickly learned, but if it's something that cramps their style, it's "What? I didn't hear that. Oh, I forgot."

The relationship between Sadie, Carla, and Ruby was interesting to watch. Carla was the nanny in every respect…care giving and loving. Ruby was more matronly. Her approach seemed to be, "We can have fun, but we must behave. We can have adventures, but we must take caution." This was okay with Carla, as they never had a spat over Sadie. Each had distinct roles to play and seemed to understand it. Ruby and Sadie photographed well. They looked awfully cute together! Holidays and family vacations offered extra interesting opportunities for fun pictures. One picture of them together in particular was taken by chance. It was a snapshot that would flash across America and turn our family upside down in a happy jumble…at least for a while.

CHAPTER ELEVEN

The Contest

In mid-September 2008, as if Ruby wasn't busy enough, Lynn noticed a contest on the back of a Milk-Bone box for "first-ever spokesdog" in their one-hundred-year history. Top prize was a $100,000 contract. All we had to do was send in a picture of one of the dogs and a family member having fun, relaxing, or being silly. Milk-Bone called it a "Milk-Bone Moment."

Lynn remarked, "Hey! What about that lucky shot you took of Sadie and Ruby at the Fourth of July parade?" The pair of cuties were both wearing sunglasses with red, white, and blue outfits. It was also Sadie's first Fourth of July in America.

We also had to write a short story about the picture. Off went the entry only to discover I used far too many words in the essay. Quickly rewritten, we sent yet another entry, just a day before the contest deadline, September 18. Enclosed was a note explaining my dumb mistake. The do-over essay would prove effective:

I'm Ruby along with my human sister and best friend, Sadie. We're both adopted. This was taken at our 4th of July parade. I was an abandoned, starving puppy, but now I'm a therapy dog with lots of friends. Life's good nowadays, and I am happy!

A week later, we received a call telling us that our entry had been accepted! Whoever was on the line tipped her hand. "Great picture and story." She wanted to talk about a password and some techy thing, so I handed the phone to Lynn. When it came to computers, I was a dinosaur. Then it was waiting time. But our lives were busy with Sadie and the dogs. The contest was soon forgotten. Our luck with such things was lousy anyway. Though Ruby was looking for something new, fun, and interesting to get involved with, she took her job as Sadie's guardian angel seriously. Demand for her volunteer work also kept her on the run. Saturday morning, October 18, our lives took a screeching turn from the daily mundane routine. Lynn had been rummaging through the spam folder on the computer when a supposed junk email caught her eye. It was dated two days prior.

Congratulations! You and your dog have been chosen as one of the top 100 Eligible Finalists in the Milk-Bone 100th Anniversary contest. Your entry will be posted on www .milk-bone.com for online voting. Voting will occur from October 19, 2008, to November 18, 2008. At the end of the online voting period, the finalist entry receiving the highest number of votes will be eligible to win the grand prize!

Wow! Out of the thousands of entries, we made the cut! Lynn's eyes welled up in a gentle cry, soft and sweet. I was like a deer in headlights, not so soft or sweet, just goofy. Sadie was napping, but the four-legged kids felt something in the air. With that cute little skip-run, Ruby led the pack into the den where we sat wondering what to do next. A plan was quickly formulated. Meanwhile, Ruby, Carla, Venus, and Molly responded to the increasing excitement. They were like minnows in a bucket; round and round they went, wiggling, mouths open in a happy smile. "Gee! What's going on?"

"Don't know, but it sure is fun!" "Okay, it's time for a good snooze."

A campaign began as if Ruby were running for office. Posters and flyers were produced: "Vote for a real American. Vote for Ruby!" Cars in parking lots, shopping malls, gas stations, innocent people on the street received Ruby's campaign materials. Media was notified. Newspapers and television got in on the action. They thought it was a fun tie-in with the presidential election!

Ruby ran a good, clean campaign, no digging up somebody else's dirty bones. She stuck to the core issue. Paws down, she should be Milk-Bone's spokesdog! Then it was over, the running, kissing, tail wagging, panting. All that was left to do was wait for the votes to be tallied, the winner to be announced, and for someone to collect that $100,000 check.

The money would sure be handy. The radio station where I worked had been sold and local broadcasting was ending, and my salary with the Duck Soup Players was reduced to less than part time because of funding issues. Within a few months, Lynn's position at her company would be eliminated after twenty-one years.

While we kidded about winning the contest, we truly never thought it would happen. Yes, we made the final one hundred, but that would be it. Then on December 10, 2008, a FedEx envelope arrived. The note inside the package read, "We are contacting you to inform you that, subject to verification of eligibility, you have been designated as one of the top three finalists in the Milk-Bone 100th Anniversary 'Make a Milk-Bone Moment' Contest."

It went on to make us promise not to tell anyone including family about this latest development. Further, Ruby and I had to be available to travel to one of three cities, New York, Chicago, or Los Angeles, on or about January 8, 2009, to participate in an on-air publicity event. The note warned us that if we leaked any details and they found out about it, we would be disqualified.

What?! Top three?! We were wildly excited. Unbelievable! Wait! They never mentioned top three before. We dug through every page of the rule book. Nothing. Hmmm, what's going on? Oh well, it didn't matter. This was great news. But to not tell family or close friends?! Ugh!

They soon knew something was up, repeatedly asking what's up with the contest. Lynn and I would smirk and say, "We're under contract and can't say a thing." That really irritated some, family especially. Then everyone had the answer. "You won, didn't you?! I just know you did!"

January 8 came and passed. Nothing. Weeks ticked by. Still nothing! We made calls, but "Shhh, we're working on it" was the only reply we received. With all the hush-hush going on, I thought we might be working with former CIA operatives. Finally, on about February 4, 2009, we got the word. It's Los Angeles!

Shortly afterward came news that it's *The Bonnie Hunt Show*! Cool. We liked her, enjoyed her movies. She's also a dog person and, like Lynn, from Chicago. We liked her talk show, too, with its play-ful, fun humor.

"When do Ruby and I leave?"

"Shhh, can't tell you that yet."

"Well, can we give our family the scoop now?"

"Shhh, not yet!"

Then on February 9 around 5 p.m. came a final word, finally! We were to leave from Minneapolis the next day at 9 a.m.! Not much notice, but hey, Ruby and I were going to Hollywood! Okay, Okay, the show was actually taped in Culver City, but who cares? Ruby and I were trading snow and ice for green grass and flowers!

In the coming days and months and years, Ruby and I would find all that glitters is not gold. The deception, the subterfuge, the false-hoods certainly would have been intriguing, if we weren't caught in the middle of it.

CHAPTER TWELVE

On to the Big Time!

Sleep was fleeting the night before we left. I hated flying, and I had not been in a plane since returning home from a USO tour in Alaska where we had had a "hard landing" at a remote military base. Just the thought of flying sent me over the edge, sweaty, clammy, heart racing, and hyperventilating with unchecked panic. Luckily, I had a secret drug: Ruby. My doctor knew that I didn't do very well on drugs. He also knew the value of service dogs for the many and varied needs of individuals. Ruby was the doctor's drug of choice. Being familiar with my needs and Ruby's background, the doctor suggested I go back to school with her and raise her to service dog standards. He wrote a prescription that was required for Ruby to attend Puppy Love School for service dogs. Certainly, her previous training and extensive experience helped her in the process. To achieve ADI standards, some tweaking was necessary, but she did very well, receiving her credentials in early 2009, just a short time before we had to fly out to California.

Having not much notice before our departure left little time for preparations, like purchasing new clothes, a suitcase, toiletries, travel dog bowls, small treats, doggie "duty" bags, a nicer collar, and other miscellaneous items. We finally finished just as the stores were closing. Then it was rush home, arrange and pack everything. Now I suppose all this could have been done a week or so before, but why get ahead of myself? Like the dogs we love, the average guy lives in the moment. And just like our furry friends, we don't multi-task all that well either. At least I didn't. I know, I know. To the men, I sound like a heretic. To the women, it's "So what's new?"

Crawling into bed late, I thought "What's the point?" The excitement was overwhelming, so was the dread and terror of flying. I counted sheep. I counted different breeds of dogs. I counted Milk-Bones. The only thing I couldn't count on was any real sleep. About the time I finally drifted off, 4:15 a.m. arrived and it was time to get up. Any grogginess I had soon evaporated as the whole family rose in a fever pitch to get ready. Last-minute items were taken care of. Checking and rechecking the suitcase, the camera, my "what to do if anything happens to me" list. Ruby seemed to know whatever was about to happen included her. She had energy to spare with that skip-running from room to room telling the pack, "Hey, I'm special today!"

On Wednesday, February 11, 2009, the limo quietly backed into our driveway at 5:30 a.m. sharp. Lee's limos, a local business bitten by the Ruby bug, had graciously offered to pick us up and deliver us to the airport. Lynn, Sadie, Ruby, and I would ride together. A quiet hush replaced our initial excited chatter. Sadie and Ruby explored the stretch limo as Lynn and I sat silently holding hands, each in our own thoughts. I was in a wild mix of emotions. Leaving Lynn and Sadie behind was difficult. After all, it was Lynn who had started this whole thing when she read about the contest on the back of a box of biscuits and suggested we enter. Suddenly my head cleared for a moment. Ruby interrupted by deciding the most comfortable spot was with her head on my lap. The thoughts continued. *What about the airport? Will they give me trouble regarding Ruby? Will they try to make her ride below? I have all the correct paperwork, but still…and flying! Arrrgghh! Nope, I am not going to think about that now. Who are the other dogs in the contest? I hope Lynn is going to be okay. Could we really win?! Whew!*

About then, the hour-long trip to the airport was over. Mary, the driver, gave Lynn her cell number to call when she was ready to leave.

"Don't get out till I put down the red carpet."

Meanwhile, other departing passengers tried to peer through the tinted windows to catch a peek at some supposed celebrity in the car. *Ha! They're about to be disappointed*, I thought.

"Hey look, hon. There's a Fox news cameraman talking to Mary. He's here for us!"

Now people were definitely interested. As we alighted from the car, I tried not to trip and fall. Lynn and Sadie looked graceful and fabulous. Ruby hopped down, proud, regal, tail wagging, with a look of "I do autographs, everybody."

As we made our way toward check-in, the cameraman in tow, I distinctly heard someone say, "I don't know, but they have to be somebody." Getting rid of the suitcase with ticket in hand, I felt better. I was down to just a small leather case, camera, and Ruby. Still, I kept checking and re-checking things. Through all my fussing, poor Lynn had the patience of a saint as I took up a position in the security line. Ruby was taking in everything, her tail a slow steady beat, like a metronome. The cameraman was about to bid us good-bye and good luck when a very familiar face popped out of the crowd. Lisa Meuwissen from *Cheaper by the Dozen*, dressed in her Northwest Airlines uniform, had come in on her day off. It was also her twentieth wedding anniversary. Lisa had known about my issues with flying and came in to help shepherd this dope through the system. Apparently, this was newsworthy as the camera started to roll again. Ruby, happy to see Lisa, wagged her tail in triple time.

Final hugs, kisses, and longing good-byes with Sadie and Lynn and I was on to the task at hand. I was next in line facing a stern-looking man checking IDs.

"Would you like the dog's ID first, sir?" I proffered.

He glanced down, giving Ruby a quick sweep.

She looked back up at him as if to say "What?!"

With no change of expression, he replied, "I trust the dog. It's your ID I want to see."

Taken aback by his comment, I fumbled for my credentials. I do believe a slight smirk traced his face when he returned them. I couldn't help but giggle.

Lisa grabbed Ruby's leash. "I'll see you on the other side of security."

"Well...but, but," and they were gone by way of the employee entrance. That Ruby was so happy to run off with Lisa was kind of startling. But then, she is a most compliant dog.

Security certainly was different than the olden days back in 1983 when last I flew. In those days, there had been none. Today there seemed to be nothing but. I hadn't been living in a vacuum. Of course I knew about the changes. It was just odd to experience them for the first time and the sad and scary reasons behind them. Left alone to my own ineptness, I managed to get through "Checkpoint Charlie" without getting arrested. On the other side, Ruby waited with Lisa, tail swinging an easy wag (the little traitor!). With plenty of time before boarding, we tried to have a leisurely breakfast. It wasn't so much for me. Panic welling up within, I wondered if the limo could still turn around. Ruby, sensing my discomfort, moved in tightly to my leg.

"Pat...Pat! Snap out of it," Lisa continued, "I've cleared it with the flight crew. You're boarding first. We'll show you around the plane, meet the crew, get you settled in."

A long pause.

"Okay, Lisa."

"Pat, you'll be just fine. Once up and flying, you'll have fun! Besides, just think why you're going."

What an angel Lisa was to come in like this on her special day. Wearing the uniform made it easier to get things done for my benefit. We had done a couple of plays together after *Cheaper*, and I considered her a friend. But this? I shall forever be grateful for the extra effort. Between Lynn and Lisa, I was spoiled rotten this day!

The flight crew was waiting for us as we passed all those waiting in line. Inside the plane, cameras came out, flight attendants posed with Ruby. Everyone, including the pilot and co-pilot, had happy, friendly faces.

Ruby was placed on the flight deck for a quick picture. In it, she clearly doesn't think it was part of the contract. As Ruby and I took our final position in a bulkhead window seat, the rest of the passengers arrived, making for a full aircraft. Ruby kept a close eye on me in the final moments before take-off. As we started to bumpily gain speed before being airborne, I gripped the seat arms, closed my eyes, and tried to breathe, terrified. In an instant, Ruby's paws were on my lap, her head tight to my chest. It was intoxicating, instantly calming. Suddenly it was all smooth, all good. Back on the floor, she continued to study my face for a minute or two before lying down and going to "screen saver mode," a name I've given a pretty cool thing she does. No matter where we are, coffee shops, restaurants, stores, when I stop, Ruby will sit a self-prescribed amount of time, between one to two minutes. If I don't move within that time frame, down she goes, fast asleep, invisible and unobtrusive.

For the first hour of the flight, the attendants stopped by about every ten minutes calling me by name to see if I needed anything. We went due west over South Dakota for a while. The pilot mentioned some towns or landmarks below. My thoughts raced back to that hot summer day and the broken axle in the motor home. It sure looked cold and desolate now, almost uninhabited. The flight plan eventually had us going southwest over Nevada and strange, empty-looking little towns and tiny abandoned airports. It would be neat to explore all that, although with my luck I'd wind up in Area 51, hauled off never to be seen again. For a while most of my fifty-nine years were washed away, replaced by a wide-eyed boy seeing things as fresh and new. Hey, Lisa was right. This is pretty fun.

In the seat to my left was an energetic young lad about eight years old. His grandma was to his left. I had been bopped, bumped, and poked numerous times the past couple of hours. One of the toys given to occupy this high-octane kid flew out of his hands and landed on Ruby. She actually opened her eyes for a second. Without hesitation, "Ricky" retrieved his toy from its position leaning against her ribs.

Finally, his grandmother spoke. "What kind of dog is that? It's unbelievably well behaved."

Trying to avoid a problem, I proffered up, "She's a service dog."

A wee bit insulted, she tried again. "I can see that with the vest it has on. What breed is it?"

Stalling just a little more, "Well, it's a female. Her name is Ruby. Ah, she's a pit bull."

Instantly, I thought I should have said boxer mix. It's worked before. We didn't need a panic at 30,000 feet. I thought, oh, God, not Duluth again! These fears zipped through my mind in a nano second.

"Aha, I thought so! Had one when I was a kid. Best dog I ever had. Nowadays they get blamed for everything, and it's not the dog's fault. If I tell someone I used to have one, they tell me I must be confused. They say I must have had a Boston terrier. They tell me there are no good pit bulls. Well, I know what I had, and Rex was the best!"

Three times during the flight, Ruby sat up, placed her head on my knees, and looked me straight in the eyes. When she was satisfied that everything was okay, it was back down for a well-deserved snooze. These check-ups were helpful, particularly during a bumpy spell that had me sweating.

As we came into Los Angeles, the scene below turned from drab brown to patches of green announcing well-manicured lawns with the attendant houses in a crazy patchwork of neighborhoods perched on hillsides, valleys, cliffs, anywhere they could take hold. Before I could gather my thoughts about dealing with my next worry, LAX, we were on the ground taxiing to the terminal. Safe! Hallelujah, luck was with me!

After a couple of quick questions about luggage claim and pick-up, I discovered I was practically on top of them. I grabbed my bag and turned around, and there was a driver holding up a sign with our name. On the way to the car, I noticed bushes with leaves and even a patch of green grass across the street. The day was sunny, and the temperature seemed to be in the low to mid-60s. Cool perhaps for LA, but to someone who's climatized for 20 below, it was downright balmy. It was now around 11:30 a.m. local time. Ruby hadn't gone potty since 4:30 our time this morning.

"Sir, do you mind if I take the dog for her business over there for just a second?"

A fast dash over and back for a piddle break, and it was time to settle into our moderately stretched Lincoln town car. I was pleased. I really don't like those monster extensions. Garish. Tasteless. Fun, perhaps, if you're going to the prom, but this was old-school

American luxury. Hmmm. Bottled water. Newspaper. Snacks. A thick, clean white towel for Ruby to curl up on should she decide to take yet another nap. But Ruby would have none of it as she sat upright, facing forward, head turned over her left shoulder looking out the window as if to the manor born.

I couldn't tell how long it took to get to the Hotel Palomar LA Westwood. It was time enough to reflect on how far Ruby and I had come. That we were actually in LA was humbling, unreal. A bit of luster was lost though, because Lynn, the person responsible for Ruby and me being here, would not be sharing the experience, except in the retelling of our story.

Arriving at the hotel, a staff member grabbed my things and carried them to check-in for me. My instructions were to tell the desk my name and who I was with.

"Oh yes sir! We've been expecting you. Milk-Bone has some gifts waiting for you."

"Oh?" looking around for them, thinking I'd just carry them up to my room.

"We'll send them right up, sir."

"That's great," I said as I hurried to catch my new friend at the elevator. The room was impeccable, stylish, and comfortable. It had a great view. Just as I was tipping the bellboy, a cart arrived loaded down with two large baskets. One for Ruby, containing all kinds of doggie treats, chewy things, and HUGE toys. The other, for me, was stuffed with wine, cheeses, meats, nuts from afar, champagne, interesting confections, and a couple of items I wasn't sure about. A search of our temporary digs turned up a fully stocked refrigerator and a packed goody drawer.

"Ruby, if we don't win, we can hold out in this room for a couple of weeks, refusing to leave." She didn't hear me. She was lying on the chaise lounge, dreamily soaking up the sun streaming in through the window. "C'mon kid, let's explore this swanky neighborhood."

About an hour into our walk around the area, a call came in. It was Cathy Coughlin, account supervisor from the IC Group out of Chicago. (They run contests and sweepstakes for large corporations.) She said that she and Jennifer Lilly, senior account executive from Coyne Public Relations out of New Jersey, would like to met Ruby and me in our room shortly. At the turn of a heel, we said good-bye to the beautifully manicured lawns of tiny but immaculate bungalows with Bentleys, Rolls Royces, and exotic sports cars of every stripe parked in the equally tiny driveways.

On the way back, we ran into one of the other top three dogs, Wyatt, the beautiful, well-muscled boxer, and his mom who seemed quite surprised to see us. She was on the cool side, but we didn't have time for small chit-chat. I would find out much later that when she saw Ruby and me she thought she didn't have a chance. She wasn't aware that I, too, felt the same about her and Wyatt. Little did we know, both of us were going to be blindsided that night.

Back in the nick of time, Ruby and I had just a few moments to prepare for this meet-and-greet.

"Be on your best behavior, girl."

With that, Ruby, lounging on the chaise again, gave a look that said, "Dad, I'm the least of your problems and leave me alone."

A knock on the door sent Ruby into a bolt-upright sitting position. As Cathy and Jennifer swept into the room, Ruby forgot all decorum in a flying leap off the couch, acting much like she did the first time we met. She was all wiggles and wild. Up on the bed, off the bed, run a few laps around the room, up and off the lounge, and back on the bed. Spinning around a few times, she finally stopped. Looking our two guests in the eyes with a confident wag of the tail, she seemed to say, "Well. What do you think? I'm cute and smart and have a great personality. Do I win? Who's the check made out to? Dad or me?"

The women looked at each other.

"Hmmm. If I smile and wiggle like a puppy, that should do the trick."

In a bit of a shock one of them stammered, "Is this Ruby or a different dog?"

I assured them this was indeed Ruby. "But, she's so small. The dog in the picture was...well...so much bigger." (Aha. That explains the supersized dog toys!)

I chuckled. "Keep in mind, the child with Ruby in that snapshot was just two-and-a-half years old. Any dog would look larger."

Clearly, they were confused and perhaps a little unconvinced. But, after a few minutes of small talk and petting Ruby, they were believers.

Something about the contest had been bothering me. Now I saw my chance to clarify it and jumped in. "I've re-read the contest rules and couldn't find anything about the final three. Was that something you folks just came up with? Or was it there from the beginning?"

I believe they both blanched and for a second time looked at each other. I was not sure who said it, but this time, the answer left me unconvinced. "Oh, it's been planned since the beginning. We just didn't want it to be common knowledge."

WHAT? This made no sense to me. But rather than pursue the issue, I let it go with an "Okay, just curious."

With that we exchanged pleasant good-byes. Cathy told me a producer from *The Bonnie Hunt Show* would be calling me later that afternoon to go over a few things and do an interview. Reminding me as they left, someone remarked, "We'll see you in the lobby at 7:30 for transport to the Wilshire Restaurant in Santa Monica. The Del Monte/Milk-Bone people will be there to meet the three finalists."

Now it was time to finish that walk. Stopping by the front desk to ask about a gift shop and batteries for my camera, I was surprised they didn't have one. Of everything checked and re-checked before I left home, batteries were not on the list. Now my camera was dead. Problem solved. "Sir, we'll get your driver in a minute." Before I knew it, Ruby and I were whisked to a drugstore about six or eight blocks away. We could have walked it for crying out loud, but it was in the opposite direction we wanted to go, so it did save time and we felt wickedly pampered.

As attentive as the staff was, they became a source of entertainment for Ruby and me. Coming or going, we simply couldn't open the front door on our own. Someone always rushed to open it for us. On occasion, it became kind of a race to see who could get to the door first. Ruby and I sneakily changed our tactics. We approached the door as if passing by toward the hotel restaurant. A door person leaped up just in case. Seeing us pass by, they'd return to their station. A sharp change in direction and we were through the door on our own terms.

Back to exploring the neighborhood, I took a few hasty pictures to document that I was really there. Hurrying back to the hotel to settle in for awhile before the producer's call, we again ran into Jacqueline, the boxer mom. Her dog, Wyatt, and Ruby pretty well ignored each other as we engaged in light conversation. More relaxed this time, Boxer Mom revealed she was a veterinarian, and that Wyatt, rescued from severe abuse, was now a doggie blood donor on a regular basis saving the lives of others. What a wonderful story this boy had to tell. Leaving his horrible past behind him, here he was, now standing by his loving forever mom on the eve of possibly becoming Milk-Bones' national spokesdog.

Hard-to-miss Winston, the Great Dane, soon joined us at the street corner. Wanting to know about the dog, I asked, "What's Winston's story?"

"Well," giggle, "my husband gave him to me as a gift. He eats a lot. Gains weight and likes to have fun." Curious about this large dog, Ruby stood in front of him, tail in that happy wag. Without warning, whack! Winston's paw came crashing down on Ruby's head. Shaking it off, she leapt to the side, then behind me. Melissa, the young woman who owned the giant, giggled. "It's okay. He's just like that. We have another smaller dog at home, and he does the same thing to him." More giggling followed. Winston was prancing in place like a race horse ready to go. We scattered and headed back to the room. Melissa, with the perfect teeth, perfect nails, perfect hair, perfect body, and perfect clothes, had her hands full with this young upstart. Walking him seemed to be an exercise in jerking the leash, pulling, being pulled, and skittering from side to side as he went where he mostly wanted to go...not very lady-like, but certainly entertaining.

Back in the room, safe from those huge paws of doom, Ruby and I relaxed, chewed on a few snacks, made a couple of calls to file a report with our supporters in the media back home, chatted with Lynn for a bit, and closed our eyes.

About the time Ruby's snoring reached a crescendo, the expected call came in. It was Kevin Boyer from Bonnie's show. He was friendly and polite. We hit it off well, spending quite a lot of time talking. He had questions about me, where I was from, my background....the usual stuff. Kevin wanted to know all about Ruby and her story. They had heard a little about her history, but he wanted the full details. Of course I had plenty to say about her but also suggested he do a search on the web when he had a chance.

"I'll just do it now."

As I continued extolling Ruby's virtues, Kevin interrupted with, "Oh my God! The stuff on her...oh my God! What a story! Bonnie is going to love her! Pat, can you send me some pictures? Any from the trip would be great as well. See what you can do, and call me back."

I called Lynn. She had received some emailed pictures taken on board the plane from Lisa. These, with a few others, were sent to Coyne PR in New Jersey who apparently had to approve them and send them on to California. I called Kevin back to let him know the pics were on the way. He had news for me as well.

"Pat, Milk-Bone had scheduled the Great Dane to appear first. Bonnie has changed it to Ruby first instead, so there's time to tell her story. She is anxious to meet her!" The significance of Milk-Bone's timing wouldn't sink in until much later as the pieces fell together.

It had been a very busy day. I looked forward to this evening with mixed feelings. I recalled from the rule book that no matter what the number of votes the winning dog received, Milk-Bone reserved the right to choose a different winner depending on a background check at the sole discretion of Milk-Bone. The potential grand-prize winner and his/her dog could be subject to an interview by the contest judges to determine the authenticity of the entry, and he/she may be disqualified if the entry has not complied with these official rules, as determined by the contest judges.

Okay then, Ruby and I will be on our best behavior. My thoughts were running wild. Aha! This is why they brought us here. The winner is obviously one of us three. But depending on what the executives see and hear in the next twenty-four hours, they may well determine a different winner.

It was time to get ready for dinner...shower, shave again, lay out my clothes, potty Ruby, call Lynn, feed and brush Ruby. We were first to the lobby. Friends and those who just know me will no doubt scoff at the idea that I was early for anything. Honestly. I don't know what happened. Something just got into me.

Informal introductions were made as the group headed to the waiting black vans out front.

Cathy from the IC group piped up. "Pat, you can't take Ruby."

"It's okay. Sure I can. She's a service dog, trained, tested to a set of standards, and certified for doing just that."

Cathy continued, now perhaps a little confused. "I don't think she's allowed."

Jennifer from Coyne PR stepped in. "Yes, she is. She can go anywhere Pat goes. Federal law." Conversation ended on that topic.

It was a longish, unremarkable drive to the Wilshire restaurant. Once there, I found it to be well-heeled casual. A class act in every way. Ruby and I stopped at the desk.

As a courteous gesture, I uttered the usual refrain, "Would you like to see the service dog's ID?"

The host was very busy. She gave a quick glance in Ruby's direction. "Not necessary, sir. Enjoy yourself!"

Once we were seated, the staff promptly removed a chair from the table, allowing Ruby to lay alongside me. At some point during my superb meal of filet mignon and grilled asparagus, the manager, an Englishman, stopped by to see us. As he introduced himself, I noted his impeccable manner of dress and great sense of color, much like my friend J. P. back home.

"I understand we have a celebrity dog here tonight." He thought of her as a Staffordshire terrier and loved the breed. After complimenting her behavior, he asked if there was anything at all they could get for Ruby. Thanking the manager profusely, I reluctantly informed him it was against the rules, but promised to save her some of my steak for later.

As the wine flowed endlessly, the mood relaxed, tongues wagged. Table talk turned to business…how Milk-Bone was purchased in the past year or so by Del Monte. Then Del Monte moved them from Pennsylvania to San Francisco in 2008. Most employees couldn't or wouldn't make the move because "Frisco" is a lot more expensive than Pittsburgh. As I understood it, these employees who couldn't included the original designers of the "Make a Moment" contest and the search for a spokesdog. These young whiz kids at our table had apparently inherited this contest. It wasn't their baby.

"Ahhh," my simple brain was at work again. This just may explain much of the disorganization and attitude we've dealt with. But what I heard next and Milk-Bone's reaction to it about rocked me back onto the floor.

Winston's dad had joined us at the table that evening. In his twenties, he was a young man with great confidence, confidence in his abilities, in his climbing the corporate ladder, in his education. He didn't mind sharing his accomplishments with any and all who would listen, perhaps just a bit of braggadocio. I started to tune him out, but when he turned to the contest, how he got in trouble for using his employer's corporate database to send out twelve thousand e-mails a day to employees asking them to vote for his wife's dog, my ears perked. I can't recall if it was his boss or human resources that brought him to task, telling him he could not use the database for personal gain.

"Ya, right, after they left I said screw them and deleted them from my list and continued sending the emails."

He thought this very funny. Boxer Mom, Jacqueline, I discovered later, was as stunned as I was. How can anybody compete with that? A manager for Del Monte foods laughed with Dane Dad.

"Well, at least you got our name out there."

Now, the rules clearly state: *Finalists are prohibited from obtaining votes by any fraudulent or inappropriate means.* But there is a hook: *as determined by sponsor in its sole discretion.* By laughing at and ignoring what Jacqueline and I believed to be a flagrant disregard for the rules, the manager was exercising Milk-Bone's "sole discretion." Dane Dad was on a roll as he went on to regale us with his and Dane Mom's adventures in cow tipping.

She protested, "I never went cow tipping."

"Yes you did, on our first date!"

"No, I didn't." She would have none of it. Unfazed, he boastfully recalled how he was caught by the cops tipping cows, didn't say if his wife was with him at the time. The manager thought this was funny, too. Gee, I thought that cow-tipping thing was debunked a long time ago.

After that, I tuned them out in exchange for some pleasant conversation with Mariana Corzo seated across from me. She was an associate brand manager with Milk-Bone. I felt Mariana was a good and honorable person. We talked mostly about kids because I brought up the difficult changes in life adopting a child at my age. I am sure she didn't know of the skullduggery going on at that time. Even with the time spent chatting with Mariana, a pall had settled in for the evening.

I was happy to return to the hotel with Ruby for a head-clearing walk. Back in the room, Ruby decided the chaise lounge was no longer adequate. The king-sized bed with an extra thick duvet and a soft pillow for her head would do nicely. With Ruby settled in, a good night call to Lynn was in order. In retelling the night's eye-opening revelations that damned blue funk took hold again. But I had to vent.

"Lynn, we didn't win. It's painfully obvious the Great Dane did. The boxer and Ruby are just window dressing."

At first Lynn thought I was kidding. I should have kept my mouth shut. By the time I was finished, Lynn was in a blue haze herself. Misery loves company, but it was wrong of me to burst the bubble. Hopes had been high with both of us now unemployed that a win would help see us through.

After our good nights and it's going to be all rights, I ordered the latest James Bond movie. Not long after the opening scene, I was in a fitful sleep, a fitful sleep in a very comfortable room, mind you. Ruby was already out and producing a light melodic snore, which was reassuring and comforting.

Thursday, February 12, dawned clear and sunny again. It was a pretty day, but I felt tired and drained. Ruby, on the other hand, was feeling unusually perky. She wasn't going to feed and potty herself. That's why she had me, and it was reason enough to get out of that supremely comfortable bed. With Ruby taken care of, it was time to shower and head downstairs to breakfast. Entering the restaurant was quite a different experience than the Wilshire the night before. The hostess who greeted us eyed Ruby suspiciously.

With a distinct accent she asked me, "Sir, are you blind?"

"No, you look great!"

Passing on my smart comment, she continued, "Sir, unless you are blind, you cannot bring that dog in here."

There is no point getting upset or angry in these situations. These are improperly trained employees who think they're doing their job. I gently explained the various types of service dogs nowadays and the federal law. "Federal law" got her attention.

"Let me show you to your seat, sir."

Although she did put us as far away as possible from everyone else, that was okay. Ruby and I needed some quiet time to make notes, prepare, and adjust attitudes for the rest of the day. At 11:00 a.m., we were scheduled for a Message Training class.

The appointed hour of 11:00 a.m. rolled around too soon, but we were ready, happy, and smiley-faced. Cathy from IC Group, Jennifer from Coyne PR, and "the manager" from Del Monte were all there. I can't recall if Mariana was present or not. The idea behind the training session was to prepare us for our national television appearance, though they did not stress that point. This was not done as a group, but each dog/owner individually. The manager, quite friendly this morning, did the interview, asking questions about Ruby and me. We went over potential questions Bonnie might ask. We covered body language, having conviction in our story, projecting confidence, not guessing or speculating on our answers. Ruby and I were given facts, figures, and a background history of the contest to study, just in case it was brought up by Bonnie. We were also warned that we couldn't say a thing to anybody about what happened on the show because it wouldn't be broadcast for a couple of weeks and we were also under contract to keep quiet.

As the session ended, like a bolt from the blue, the manager said, "Pat, you and Ruby represent better than anyone here, the ideal, the spirit of what the Make a Moment contest is all about!"

What?! Were my gut feelings that far off? Usually I was pretty good at reading people. Lynn told me this all the time. Shocked, stunned, and speechless didn't begin to cover my feelings. I took this as a tip-off that Ruby had won! I was over the moon! In all the excitement, a couple of contracts quickly came out of nowhere. I'm sure someone told me what they were for, but I paid no attention as my mind was wild with anticipation. I didn't read them in any detail, instead saying, "I trust you people" as I signed God knows what. I did not receive a copy of the contracts. Dumb, dumb, dumb! My excuse would be that I was so excited by what had just happened. In retrospect, it was pretty sneaky.

But for now, I was thrilled. Panting to get back to the room and call Lynn, I bid everyone good-bye, promising to see them in the lobby at 3:30 for transport to *The Bonnie Hunt Show*. The call to Lynn was short. "Hon, I think we won." I went on to give a short version of the class, highlighting the important parts. What a 180 from last night! The poor woman must have thought I went off the deep end.

Things were running late that afternoon as we finally left sometime after 4:00 p.m. Tension was almost unbearable. I don't recall much conversation in our black van on the long ride to the studio, but maybe it was just me, lost in my own thoughts. Along with that tension was true excitement. That kid in me was back. Ruby didn't have a care in the world, peacefully sleeping most of the trip except to check on me occasionally. At last, we were here, the Culver City Studio on West Washington Boulevard in Culver City. Rolling up to the guard shack, I noticed a long line of people who were I assumed, waiting to get in as audience members.

As back in Minneapolis, heads were bobbing, perhaps to see somebody rich or famous riding with us. By this time things were getting surreal for me. We rolled up to a side door and were hustled in to meet various producers. They told us to relax, get something to eat if we'd like, and they would soon be with us as they were taping another Bonnie Hunt segment before ours. Okay then! Let's take a look at that food! Well, there was plenty of it, including what appeared to be Chicago dogs and Dad's Root Beer. I had heard that Bonnie's Chicago roots run deep, and this was proof positive. That and half her crew were wearing Cubs caps or jackets.

But something was wrong. I wasn't hungry. Wasn't hungry?! That was not like me. I didn't have stage fright. I had done too many stage plays, industrial training, and educational films over the years. So that wasn't it. Perhaps it was that doubt was creeping back in. I resigned myself to visiting the large green room, its floor completely covered in plastic sheets. I guess the specter of nervous dogs making mistakes on the lovely carpeting was a genuine concern.

Relatives of Winston and Wyatt waited along with a number of people who were curiously just there. I had no clue who they were. A couple of minutes with Winston's antics sent Ruby and me scurrying out of the room. It was time to wander the hall ways and try to stay out of everybody's way. Almost immediately we ran into model/actress Molly Sims. She cooed over Ruby for a few moments saying she had a Yorkie at home. As quickly as we met, she was carted off by a staff member to prepare for her appearance on our show.

It was now between show tapings. Even so, it was obvious the crew was still on a very controlled schedule. Yet everyone was happy and having a good time. Also they were kind, respectful, and interested in their guests, including we three Milk-Bone finalists. Suddenly, out of all the tumult, there was Bonnie wearing a black suit, looking great! She warmly introduced herself with a positive handshake, then went directly for Ruby down at her level on the floor. No pretense here! Bonnie has the same effect on animals as Lynn. They loved her and even, as in Ruby's case, temporarily forget some of their training, as she surrendered herself completely to all the petting Bonnie had to offer. Up off the floor, Bonnie said, "Just a minute, Pat," and she disappeared, returning a few moments later with a hand-written note to Ruby and me.

I had met a fair number of celebrities over the years between the USO and my radio show. Some had me sadly disillusioned after their appearance. I had never met one as richly warm, approachable, kind, humble, and just plain nice as Bonnie Hunt. This is probably why we never hear anything scandalous about her. I'm sure that the loyal employees who surrounded her would concur.

In my travels around the building, I passed by the Milk-Bone people. The manager was talking about balloons dropping from the ceiling and a still photographer taking pictures during the show. I sauntered into the dressing room in time to witness Winston causing more chaos. Finally, they had to remove him for a walk outside. He was a handsome boy, but young and wild. I'm sure he felt the tension, too. But his age and lack of training came into play. The poor fellow just couldn't handle it. This was simply my opinion.

The pace was quickening now. Hair and makeup people grabbed me in a futile attempt to make me look at least somewhat presentable for television. They were as nice as everybody else around there and did their best, but as I left, I thought I heard one whisper to a co-worker, "We tried, but damn, at least the dog looks great."

It was on to rehearsal. We three finalists and the dogs were led backstage where a floor director put us in our proper order of appearance. At the risk of bragging, Ruby was at home. Comfortable, confident, and happy, she was used to this backstage routine. We waited. Every time the band kicked in it was loud, frightening Wyatt some but especially Winston. He jumped, spun, and moved about making his mom look like a rag doll. Bang! The band started in again. It was Ruby and me tossed out onto the set. Ruby's stride was on and supremely smooth. It was a huge set! Another floor director showed us our mark.

The band members, elevated and slightly to the right, looked down, smiling at her. Ruby returned the gesture by looking directly at them wagging her tail almost to the beat. "So what's up, fellas, is that going to be my intro?" Seeing that, some of guys started to laugh. I was enormously proud of my little Ruby so far from her rough start in that empty house. Sometimes when she dreams, Ruby makes pitiful whimpers and cries. Dreaming of the bad old days? I hope not. Today, win or lose, is Ruby's day. A few more instructions were given, and the other two finalists came out.

Then it was time to go back to the green room as the real taping was about to begin. We would have to wait awhile as the Milk-Bone segment was to be at the end of the show. Restless, I decided to walk the halls again when Cathy and Jennifer approached me. I can't recall the conversation verbatim, but the gist was that they, Milk-Bone, had locked horns with Bonnie Hunt's people, who didn't want this to be a Milk-Bone commercial. Apparently some things would not be allowed. Clearly, the contest manager, the public relations people and Del Monte/Milk-Bone executives were not happy. They asked if I could mention the contest and of course Milk-Bone as much as I could when out there on air. They probably asked the other two finalists the same thing.

Suddenly it was show time! Get ready! The manager from Milk-Bone had a last-minute request that whoever wins, the other two be happy for them. Congratulate them as well. Once again we were led behind the set. This time, however, it was shhh, quiet please. The audience applause and band set Ruby up for fun. Like her play years before at Lakeshore, she was pumped and ready to go on. The floor director, an Australian, had his hand on my shoulder as if we were at the starting gate of a race.

Back from a commercial break, Bonnie did the setup: "*Welcome back folks. In honor of their 100th anniversary, Milk-Bone held a contest searching for the dog who will be their first-ever spokesdog. Thousands of entries were narrowed down to 100. And America voted it down to three based on the story each dog had to tell. The winner is going home with $100,000. That's a lot of money! Let's meet the first finalist. Please welcome Pat and his dog, Ruby.*"

The words, "Now! Go!" produced a mega-watt of electricity for us as we practically charged out to meet Bonnie again. Compared to the rehearsal's smooth entry, Ruby was racing to get out on stage. Okay, I'll admit, me too. I tripped slightly as Ruby bumped into me. Of course it was caught on tape! As you might expect, Bonnie greeted Ruby first, as it should be!

She asked, "What makes Ruby so special?"

I gave a short version of how she was found and fostered, how these foster dogs seem to appreciate their new lives. We covered her therapy work. Ruby looked great on television. She was back to cool, calm, and confident.

Next thing I knew, Bonnie was on the floor with Ruby. For her part, Ruby was tenderly loving it. She leaned against Bonnie giving her sweet little kisses.

"Oh, snuggle pup!" Bonnie was clearly enamored with Ruby, gently petting and stroking her. She went on, while still on the floor, to ask about how Ruby, now as a service dog, helped me fly again. When described what it was she did on the plane for me, the audience applauded. A picture of the two of us on the plane flashed across the screen. At the end of our allotted time, Bonnie added, *"This is the way we know pit bulls when you know the truth. They're just gentle souls, and I feel badly they get such a bad rap. But Ruby can change that along with Milk-Bone recognizing her and how sweet she is."*

I took my place on the second mark. Total air time: Two minutes, twenty one seconds.

Next it was Winston's turn to come out. I waited smugly for the explosion. Whoa! Hold on a minute! Did they switch dogs? This guy came out like a gentleman. I can't say if someone gave him something to settle down, but his behavior was far different than it had been the past couple of days. Unlike Ruby, he didn't pay attention to Bonnie. Still, even if a bit nervous, he was doing well enough out there on stage. When asked about his story, his mom, Melissa, said, they got him at seven weeks old. He was just ten pounds and the tiniest little thing. He started growing and gaining five to ten pounds per week. It was just crazy! Giggle. They rented a vehicle to drive from Wisconsin. By the second day, Winston was done. They had to lure him back into the car with a Milk-Bone. It was just

121

crazy! Giggle. Total air time: One minute, twenty-five seconds.

Wyatt and his mom Jacqueline's turn was next. Perhaps just a shade uneasy, Wyatt, wide-eyed and beautiful, still cut a handsome figure. With his swagger and all-around wider body including a very thick neck, he'd look malevolent if it weren't for such a sweet face. Unfortunately, time was running down. Bonnie had Jacqueline cut to the chase on Wyatt's current hero's work as a regular blood donor, saving other dogs' lives, his being a rescue from a cruelty case. Then back to blood donation and that there are facilities available in each state to donate as well. Boxer Mom had the least amount of time but packed in some good information. Total air time: One minute, five seconds.

Now the time had come. The months of waiting. The false starts and stops. It was the moment of truth. Would our lives change? How many house payments should we make if we won? But first a commercial break! Bonnie led us out. *"After the break, we'll come back and announce which of the dogs will get the $100,000!"*

Too quickly, we were back as Bonnie picked it up. *"Each of the runner-ups will be getting a lifetime supply of Milk-Bones and their dogs will be featured on the Milk-Bone box. This is very exciting. Drum roll please. Here we go! The winner is Melissa's dog, Winston!"*

Pow! Zap! Thonk! Like the old *Batman* television series, I could just about see those words in full color above the set. I felt pummeled as my heart sank to the floor. If we had lost to the Boxer, okay, at least he had something going, a real story. But Winston's dad's attitude and using that corporate database stuck in my craw.

We found out later that Winston had beaten Wyatt and Ruby by only four or five hundred votes even with that email edge. We had the moral victory. I guess that's worth something. My mind was racing at warp speed now. Despite shallow breathing and shaking, I was determined to be a sport about it, congratulating Melissa.

"How can I tell Lynn? What are we going to do? Ruby, you are a perfect little partner!" My thoughts were in a jumble now as the oversized check was handed to Winston's mom. I had thought there may be a smaller surprise check for the runners-up, but there was nothing.

Bonnie ended our segment. *"Thank our guests and these great dogs and their owners. We were talking during the break, and it's so important to rescue an animal if you have the love and the time and just share that moment if you can. If you can't take the dog home, go and volunteer at a place for a couple of hours a week. Right?"*

I answer, *"Absolutely!"* Bonnie continued, *"And blood donation is so important."*

Funny thing was, Melissa nodded her head in affirmation as Bonnie spoke about rescue. I had been given the feeling our dogs were little second-class mutts that must be tolerated by Winston's family.

After the cameras stopped taping, Bonnie came over. Petting Ruby first, she turned to me with a good, solid cheek-to-cheek hug. "Pat, I am so sorry. I wanted a rescue dog to win. I wanted you and Ruby to win."

I asked if I could get the outtakes shot during breaks and after the show ended as the cameras continued to roll for awhile. Somebody in the control booth liked Ruby. I had noticed a lot of fun shots of her on the monitors.

Bonnie turned to one of her people. "Please get him all the outtakes and a copy of the show before he leaves."

The manager from Milk-Bone overheard us and jumped all over that one! Apparently he must have thought I was a security risk.

"NO! He can't have anything until after the show is aired! Pat, once the show is aired, we'll send you a copy of the show and prints of the pictures taken during the taping."

I never received the outtakes, the pictures, or a copy of the show. Nothing. I have repeatedly asked Milk-Bone for them, and have never received a reply.

Shell shocked, I made my way back to the green room. Winston and his family were celebrating. Jacqueline, her mom, and one or two other people as I recall, planned to go out for a quiet dinner. Retreating to my now favorite haunt, the hallway, we bumped into Cathy and Jennifer.

They were looking a little sad. "Pat, this isn't the outcome we would have liked, but..." They stopped short of saying who they thought should have won. They did, however, brighten our spirits by showing us a mock up Milk-Bone box with a great picture of Ruby on the front. They wouldn't allow me to take it home with me. "We'll send it to you later." Wyatt would get his own box as well. "The boxes should be out this late spring or summer."

By this time, Winston was acting like the dog I knew. "There's going to be trouble with this one," one of them said.

We excused ourselves, saying we'd meet them at the van for transport back to the hotel. Ruby and I popped out the side door for a breath of fresh air. As we descended the stairs, I noted a crowd had gathered. I presumed they were waiting for wrestling star Jerico or Molly Sims. The crowd started to applaud! I turned to look behind us. Nobody! People started to call out. "Can we pet Ruby?" What in the world? "We wanted Ruby to win!" "She should have won!" More shouts. Emotions lay bare, my eyes welled with tears.

"Ruby. You've won hearts and gathered fans. I told you this would be your day!" We practically flew down the rest of the steps to do an impromptu hands-on meet-and-greet. It was wonderful.

The ride back to the hotel was long and silent. Winston's family had taken a different transport. Wyatt's mom and company went out for dinner. That left Cathy and me on the front bench seat. Ruby snuggled between us sound asleep. Cathy began to caress her softly. I was surprised by the tender display from someone so corporate, but it was obvious she was an animal lover. You never know what's beneath the surface. It was nice to see. Jennifer sat quietly in the seat behind us. The silence in the van was only broken by an occasional sniffle. This raised questions. Were they truly saddened by the out-come? Or was there something deeper going on? Did Ruby win, but was rejected because of her breed?

I recalled a conversation in late January with an acquaintance who happened to be a lawyer and a cynic of corporate America. "Pat, don't get your hopes up. Even if Ruby gathered the most votes, she would lose the contest. Milk-Bone is not going to have a pit bull as a spokesdog, no matter what nice things she's done. Get a grip on reality. They are not going to risk a public relations fiasco."

Good point, and I suppose I should have been grateful Ruby was allowed to come this far. I had no idea if his conspiracy theory held water. But it makes some sense. If indeed that was the case, at least they didn't rub our nose in it, unlike Dane Dad and his ballot box stuffing. But there were more important things to attend to at the moment, like breaking the news to Lynn. In my call to her early this afternoon, I had been so positive about our winning.

We pulled up at the hotel as Cathy and Jennifer asked if they could take us to dinner. We arranged to meet at the hotel restaurant in thirty minutes. Back up to the room to freshen up, I considered calling home. Thinking it through, I knew it would take more time than I had. Later would be better.

Just sitting down for a quiet dinner, I was thrilled to see Melissa, her husband, and her parents saunter over to the table. "Mind if we join you?" They sat down.

Cordial as I could be, it was difficult to swallow Dane Dad's droning on about his accomplishments again. This time there was no talk about his use of the database. Then he started in about Melissa's not cooking, not knowing what a crock pot was when she received one as a gift. My sympathies were with her. I had enough. Choking down the rest of my dinner, I excused myself, lamenting how tired I was.

After completing Ruby's bedtime duties, the phone call to Lynn couldn't be put off any longer. Still, I continued to putter around the room. It wasn't that I feared her anger. I knew she wouldn't be. That came later as she was given the full details. The breaking of her heart was what killed me. Finally, far too late into the evening, I placed the call. Already in bed, half-asleep, Lynn was shocked at the news we lost. It was a difficult conversation, best left unrecalled. The next morning, we had a 10:15 a.m. flight home. After I hung up with Lynn, I was anxious to get home with its lovely slippery ice, snow, bitter wind chills, and gray-and-white landscape. I packed everything but the essentials. Sleep would be as elusive as the night before I came to California. Morning dawned gray with spotty rain showers. "How flipping fitting is this," I grumbled, tending to last-minute details before heading down to the limo. Though now, far more confident about going through LAX, I had called to be picked up at the hotel a half-hour earlier than scheduled. Downstairs, the staff was up to their usual attentive standards, carrying things, asking if there was anything else they could possibly do, offering to take care of a bag containing Ruby's ahh, um, doo doo.

Getting through ticketing and baggage drop-off was a breeze, thanks to a kind, very helpful Northwest flight attendant. Now

Ruby and I were alone to run the security gauntlet. Forgetting things in my coat pockets, my shoes, and my belt buckle kept me running back to grab another tub, then another until I had four scattered down the line. Ruby and I proceeded through the metal detector. BEEP, BEEP, BEEP. Ruby's tags, collar adornments, and other metal paraphernalia set off the alarms loud and clear!

"Sir!" a serious young man barked. "Could you stand over here, please."

We quickly complied. "Sir, could you point to your tubs?" Knowing we'd done nothing wrong, I wasn't worried, just concerned about missing my flight "Ah, sure. That one. That one, and that one."

"So then you have three tubs?" I had forgotten about my cell phone by itself in a tub.

"Oh no! There's one more. There! It's my cell."

Clearly, this young man, whom I judged to be a new hire, was satisfied to catch someone who had slipped up. "So you're telling me you don't have three tubs. You have four tubs."

"Yes, yes, that's right." I believe they pulled my tubs for closer scrutiny.

"You see I really haven't traveled that much and..."

He cut me off short. "Could you please follow me, sir?" Oh! Oh! This seems to be getting serious. He led us to a small glassed-in room segregated from the other passengers. The fresh-faced young fellow considered Ruby and me for a few moments. He seemed to not know what to do next. "I need to get my supervisor." With that he disappeared, returning around five minutes later with a middle-aged man.

A seasoned professional, his face showed years of experience. Not saying much, he studied Ruby closely. Finally he spoke. "Mind if I pat down your dog?"

I almost burst into laughter, but remained cool. "No, not at all."

A little hesitant, he asked, "It won't bite, will it?"

I wasn't sure why he just didn't have me remove the vest and hand it to him for inspection. Perhaps he thought it might be a bomb. "No. You're okay. She's a service dog."

Once down on the floor, he carefully felt the outside of her vest. Next came slipping his hand under the vest, slowly feeling every square inch. If the supervisor was worried about Ruby's reaction, he needn't be. Her eyes were closed, enjoying this unexpected massage. Convinced Ruby represented no threat to domestic air travel, he stood up. Still, he kept looking her over.

"What breed of dog is that?"

Damn! Here's that question. I was forthright. She's a pit bull.

His reaction was swift and to the point. "Jesus! I thought so! Wait till I tell my wife I patted down a pit bull today! I'm seeing it, but I don't believe it." With that I did a little pit bull history lesson. But it was Ruby herself that left them converts.

Free at last, we zipped up the nearby stairs. With plenty of time to spare, Ruby and I had a leisurely breakfast at Burger King. Our boarding gate was right next door. As we were shuffling onto the crowded plane, I thought Lisa could have had the decency to come out to California to see Ruby and me through security and on to our seat, but then I wouldn't have a great story to tell!

The plane ride back home would be far different than going out. Oh, the flight was glass smooth. No turbulence. The turbulence was in the plane. Our seat assignment was screwed up. Instead of a bulkhead seat with at least some space for Ruby, we sat behind a row of seats that had nothing in front of them. The large empty space was because of a door located there. We were on the aisle with no space for Ruby and my legs. Topping it off was that the plane was packed. I pleaded with a flight attendant, asking if there was an outside chance something else might be available or, if perhaps, I could switch with someone.

Busy, not wanting to be bothered, and without a hint of warmth or concern, her answer left no gray area and no hope. "You'll just have to put your dog under the seat in front of you." I had Ruby lay on her side and slid her under the seat as ordered. God bless the little trooper—she stayed without protest, coming out only when I called her for a bit of a stretch.

This caused my right foot to protrude just slightly into the aisle. The flight attendants were alert. Within seconds I was being called sir again. "You must remove your foot from the aisle."

I protested. "But I'm giving Ruby a chance to stretch out a bit. It can't be comfortable under that seat."

Unmoved, she repeated herself firmly. This time we quickly followed orders. The rest of the flight continued without incident, Ruby and I watching our Ps and Qs. We were painfully cramped and so very happy when we landed. As we disembarked the plane in Minneapolis, two of the crew including Ms. Vigilant thanked us for flying with them and said that they had never seen such a well-behaved dog. I was left speechless.

Lynn and Sadie, dressed to the nines, flowers in hand, were waiting for us at baggage claim. Lynn's warm welcome hid her disappointment well. I offered to drive home, but she wouldn't hear of it.

"You can start driving tomorrow. Relax!"

So Ruby and I were chauffeured one last time. Instead of a black limo, we rode in a black eight-year-old Pontiac Aztec. Oh well, the way things have been going since last night's taping, I was lucky it was not a Yugo.

During the time between Ruby's homecoming and the date *The Bonnie Hunt Show* aired on February 23, friends and family speculated that we had won. But they wanted to know for sure. They tried baiting us, tripping us up, catching us off-guard, and plain old-fashioned wearing us down. One family member even became angry. Through it all, we remained steadfast and mysterious.

Media attention continued, accumulating with an almost full-page picture of Ruby in the St. Paul *Pioneer Press*. After the air date, people were shocked by the winner. No one knew what to say at first, until they learned of the database caper.

About a week after the show aired, a call came in from Jennifer at Coyne Public Relations. "Pat, have you been reading the emails to *The Bonnie Hunt Show*?" I hadn't. "Pat, America loves Ruby! Go read them!"

Wasting no time I went to the show's website. Reading Ruby's praises first, I went on to others that made some important points. Others still were mean-spirited about Winston. That he won the way he did was not his fault. Heck, it wasn't even Melissa's doing. The bottom-line email theme of comments to the show had some pretty good points.

"Milk-Bone blew a PR person's dream opportunity to use all three dogs in a great campaign. Winston a regular dog as the spokes-dog, Wyatt, a blood donor as the hero dog, and Ruby as the service dog. Also, there should have been three cash prizes."

I certainly wouldn't argue that!

Meanwhile, there were plenty of things to keep us busy. The contest was over. It was time to move on and wait for Ruby's picture to appear on the front of those boxes at the local store. But hold on here! Milk-Bone decided to mix things up a bit. In the coming months, a spin or two left us shaking our heads.

But everything would pale when cancer came a-calling on Ruby. My world was turned upside down. If Lynn and I thought the tumult in our family from the contest was winding down, life once again had other plans.

CHAPTER THIRTEEN

Life Goes On…None Too Quietly!

All too soon it was May 2009. Every week we'd go to the market expecting to see Ruby's cute little face looking back at us. The ninety days mentioned by Milk-Bone as the timeline for the new boxes to be produced was now here. But there was nothing. Calling them was futile. No response. The media in the Twin Cities was doing a follow-up on exactly when the boxes would appear. I had to stall. It would be the first of many. Finally word came down that the boxes would be out in August or September.

Okay, we could work with that quite nicely. For the past three years in early September, Ruby had been giving obedience demonstrations with Total Recall School for Dogs at the Minnesota State Fair. She was always popular with the vast majority of people. In between demonstrations Ruby was available to meet the public. By the end of the day, she was lucky to have any fur left from all of the petting. Of course, from time to time, there were a few of those individuals who had to make crass comments about her breed. Paying them no attention was always the best policy. What a coup it would be to have a Milk-Bone booth where Ruby could be stationed, looking dignified and handing out product samples. The topper would be stacks of "Ruby Boxes" on display. Around 1.5 million people pass through the gates each year at the state fair. This would be a great public relations event for Milk-Bone.

The media would be happy to cover it. By now they were following her life and adventures pretty well. Contacting Jennifer at Coyne PR, she liked the idea, told us to put a proposal together, send it to her, and she'd pass it on to Milk-Bone. We never heard a word back from them...an opportunity missed.

Ruby was too busy to be offended: volunteering with her seniors, camping, personal appearances, and posing for a calendar. She even took time to do another play, *Moon Over Miami,* with her friends J.P. Barone and Lisa Meuwissen. In it, Ruby played a flea-bitten stray picked by a female Dennis the Menace–type character on her way to stay with her older aunt and uncle. A pair of curmudgeons, they weren't any too happy to see the dog.

Ruby tried to expand her work to kids' hospitals. It made perfect sense. Having worked with kids before, she had a gentle disposition with them. Plus she had a natural affinity for those who were ill.

We decided to go to Gillette Children's Hospital in St. Paul where the Duck Soup Players had started forty years before. Besides, the parents of a child who spent a lot of time at Gillette asked Ruby to visit their daughter. I dropped off a stack of newspaper articles, a DVD of television news stories, therapy and service dog credentials, and personal references. It was all there. A few weeks later a letter arrived saying, "Looks like you have a nice dog there, but no pit bulls." St. Paul Children's Hospital gave us a rebuff as well. We could understand the concern, but to be dismissed outright was frustrating!

Around May, Lynn noticed a small lump on Ruby's left hind leg. In short order, she was in an examination room at Stillwater Animal Hospital, a highly regarded clinic. Dr. Jen Urban didn't think much of the lump, but took a sample for a peek under a microscope.

Nothing unusual was found. The growth was drained, and we were sent on our way.

By now Milk-Bone was at it again. The boxes would not be coming out at the end of summer. "There is going to be a photo shoot for all three top dogs rumored to be in either New York or Chicago." This was to be done for a consistency of backgrounds and picture quality. Then it was time to wait for the when and where details. Meantime, we had a vacation planned!

Just before we left for the Dakotas in mid-July, I called Milk-Bone as a precaution to see if the shoot was close at hand. It wasn't. The trip was relaxing, interesting, fun, and uneventful other than meeting a lot of curious people with the same old questions about Ruby. That was okay, though. We just considered them educational opportunities. The only twist was taking pictures of her in goofy situations with the digital camera that each of the first one hundred finalists won in the Milk-Bone contest. I would turn these pictures into fun make-a-moment posters, sending them to all those connected with Milk-Bone. "They'll love it!" With some volunteer help from a graphic designer, the great-looking posters were sent out. I don't know what Milk-Bone thought. I never heard a word back from them. But the public loved them at various events where Ruby was a guest. Quite a few were produced for fans of the little diva.

Returning from Ruby's Dakota adventures, an email awaited us. The photo shoot was on for August 21 in Chicago!

In early August, that pesky lump returned on Ruby's leg. Back to the vet, it was drained again. Once more a small sample was run under a microscope. Dr. Jen said things looked okay but warned that if it started to grow larger or bother Ruby, it should be removed. The word cancer wasn't used. Dogs get lumps. I certainly wasn't concerned. Time flew by. Before we knew it, the photo shoot was upon us.

Compared to the California trip, the trek to Chicago was certainly more subdued, yet fun with none of the pressure. While I still didn't like flying, the flight in both directions was pleasant with good seats and a great flight crew. I was really starting to enjoy airports with the vastly interesting variety of people. Again, a limo picked us up for the ride to our hotel.

"You know, Ruby, I guess I could get used to this."

From her upright, forward-facing position, she barely glanced in my direction. "I am used to this," she seemed to say.

We arrived at the Hard Rock Hotel on Michigan Avenue in the early evening, around 7:00. Milk-Bone must be given kudos for its selection of hotels—another great place with a first-rate staff. A note said we had the evening to ourselves. In fact, we had till tomorrow afternoon free...no corporate execs, no meetings, no pressure.

I loved Chicago, the theaters, the museums, the stores, the many great restaurants! I had been here five or six times before, and it was always exciting to return. The on-and-off rain that night cut short our downtown stroll, but the next morning Ruby and I were up early, off to a coffee shop around the corner. We then took time for a nice, long walk. With another poster in mind, I took plenty of pictures. This time instead of goofy or fun, she looked mostly regal or upscale. Hmmm, I guess Ruby is getting used to the good life!

We spent the better part of the day enjoying "the city with the big shoulders" until it was time to get back for departure to the shoot. Seeing Wyatt from a distance, Ruby went on alert for a moment. A second later her tail wagged furiously as she recognized the manly lug. "Hi, Wyatt! Funny to see you here! What's going on?" A little tail wag or two on his part was followed by his playing hard to catch. I would say he was a bit stuffy. I guess he didn't want the reputation as "easy." A few minutes were spent exchanging pleasantries with his mom and her boyfriend, when Winston

134

and his parents arrived at the large van that would carry us all to the photo studio. Winston greeted Ruby with a growl and a lunge, narrowly missing her. He was hurriedly stuffed behind the rear seat, while Ruby and I cowered up front.

All of us were expecting a large corporate studio of some kind. Imagine our surprise after a very long ride when we rolled up to Pink Parrot Photo in a strip mall in Naperville. One collective gasp said it all! It was not lost on the manager from Milk-Bone. He jumped in, saying, "Candice has a great reputation and has worked with *National Geographic* and others as well."

The photos on the walls of the waiting room spoke volumes of her abilities. "But we'll see," I whispered to Ruby. "The manager" decided that Ruby should go into the studio first, "since she is the easiest to work with."

It wasn't but a couple of moments and I was convinced this twenty-something woman had deep talent. She really knew how to light a brindle as she fell in love with Ruby. Candice spent a lot of time with her. "She's just so incredibly expressive! So photogenic! Ruby is just giving me so much!"

The only fly in the ointment was that Winston's dad decided he needed to be in the studio with us, yammering on and on with another Milk-Bone person about how Chicago loved Winston or some such thing. Everyone else was courteous and stayed in the waiting room.

As one might expect of a celebrity pooch, Winston was a very pampered dog. I couldn't recall the details of his daily grooming routine, but did note that his parents carried in a very nice, soft bed so he wouldn't have to lie on the "dirty floor" while he waited. Ruby, who was plenty pampered herself, also took note from her perch on high as she sat on the vinyl-covered chair next to me. Winston's turn came last.

As the tip of his long tail disappeared through the door, Ruby looked at me. She liked nothing more than something fluffy, soft, and comfortable. With that "Dad, can I?" look, I knew what she wanted.

"Okay," I said. Gingerly she hopped down, gave the bed a quick sniff, circled a few times, snuggled in, and was fast asleep within a minute. Sometime later with the rodeo over in the studio, Winston and his parents burst back through the door catching Ruby in the middle of her catnap. Without planning a clever response, I launched into an apology. "I'm sorry, but the bed looked so tempting to Ruby." Then I took it a step beyond. "But you might not want to let Winston sleep on it until it's washed. Ruby picked up some sand fleas in the past couple of days or so and by the time I noticed she was infested it was too late to get her treated before we left for Chicago." At the word "infested," I thought poor Melissa was going to faint. "Just kidding! Just kidding! No fleas." My quick wit was not particularly appreciated. They were, however, relieved.

Just before the group left, the Milk-Bone people reviewed the photo session pictures. I wasn't able to squeeze behind the front desk quickly enough as everybody jammed in place to take a peek as well. Ruby's pictures came up first. "The manager's" comments that echoed Candice's had me dancing on the ceiling. "Oh my God, she is beautiful! Oh my God, look at that! She's so photogenic!" I tried to stretch my neck to see, but couldn't. No matter. I'll see them later. Right now I was bursting my buttons! I took Ruby outside for a potty break as proud as could be.

When we returned, everyone was standing around the van saying their good-byes to the Milk-Bone executives. "The manager" said that when they were done picking the pictures they wanted, he would send each of us a disk of the rest of the pictures of our dogs. (We never received them.)

Boxer Mom Jacqueline started querying him about the boxes. When are they coming out? And is each of the dogs still going to get their own box? I carefully watched "the manager" who, for the first time, was clearly uncomfortable, looking down then away before answering.

"Well, there was some talk about having all the dogs' pictures on one box," quickly adding before we retrieved a rope, "but I think there will still be individual boxes. They'll be out in about ninety days." I thought, Oh no, not the dreaded ninety-day mantra again! With that they told us we had the night free, then bid us good-bye.

That evening, per Jacqueline's suggestion, Ruby and I went to Morton's Steakhouse. What a great place! Not so much for its décor, which was certainly upscale, but for the food and service! Our server stopped by the table every three or four minutes asking me by last name how everything was or if she could get me anything. She also asked how Ruby was doing. A couple who had been seated next to us while we waited for dessert heard the waitperson ask how we were. Unable to see Ruby, the gentleman asked, "Do you have a service dog there?"

I answered, "Yes, sir," hoping he wouldn't inquire about the breed. He didn't, as he praised the unseen dog.

"You'd never know it was there. Now that's great training!" Ruby was lying under the table opposite the couple. Partially obscured by the long tablecloth, she was waiting silently and unobtrusively for a little piece of the steak bounty I had surely saved for her later pleasure in a doggie bag.

We paid our bill and started to leave when the gentleman next to us about choked on his vegetables when he saw Ruby. "That's a pit bull!"

I started down that familiar path of "Yes, but..."

He stopped me short. "You don't have to sell me. We have

several friends who own them. Great dogs, but they get a bad rap. But I never heard of one as a service dog." His female companion asked if they could take a picture.

"Of course you can." It was a pleasant end to a lovely evening.

The next morning broke clear and sunny. By 6:30, Ruby and I were packed and ready to go. Because our flight didn't leave until late morning, we had time for a scone and coffee at the shop around the corner, followed by a brisk walk. Along the way, we met a nice Chicago cop. He was curious about Ruby. He asked a lot of questions, and we left him shaking his head in disbelief at our answers as we hurried back to meet the limo.

Arriving just in time to gather my bags from behind the desk and say good-bye to the fun staff, we ran into Winston and Melissa returning from his potty break. In front of astonished employees and guests, he greeted Ruby with a powerful roar and another lunge. Tugging and pulling at his leash attached to a sparkling new pinch collar, I assumed Melissa was embarrassed as she didn't look at me or anybody else as she struggled to get him out of the lobby. This was getting old. I was going to call them on it. But why? We were never going to see him again. I thought that maybe he just doesn't like small dogs until Jacqueline said Winston did the same thing to Wyatt.

It is interesting to note that, during the original spokesdog contract period that ran through the entire year of 2009, Milk-Bone never used Winston for anything—no public appearances or events.

Back home, the contest behind us, things settled into an easy rhythm again, until one day I noticed Ruby biting at that left rear leg. Feeling it, the lump had returned, larger than before. Back to the vet, she suggested that it be removed. Still, cancer was not suspected.

Imagine my frozen terror when Dr. Jen of solemn voice called to say the biopsy was back. It was indeed cancer. She went on to explain what type it was. But I only heard about every fourth or fifth word she said. My mind was racing, spinning, bending, not wanting to accept the word cancer. Not my Ruby! My God, this can't be happening! Not to my Ruby! The doctor tried to be optimistic, but when I picked up the histology report, I wasn't encouraged. It read in part, "The growth pattern, atypia, mitotic activity and presence of two separate masses are worrisome for a low-grade malignancy. The findings are not consistent with a hemangiosarcoma."

Also, there were tentacles spreading out from the tumors. This could be expensive. I was only getting paid part time with the Duck Soup Players. Lynn still hadn't found work. We were struggling just to keep our little house let alone pay for cancer treatments. With nowhere to turn, we were devastated.

A businesswoman from New York who had been following Ruby stepped forward to pay for all of Ruby's medical expenses. She apparently considered Ruby to be one of the most important dogs of her breed in the country. This anonymous angel also referred us to top-gun animal oncologist Dr. Jerold Post from New York City to take a look into Ruby's case. A graduate from the University of Minnesota, Dr. Post worked together with Ruby's primary-care veterinarian and the university to come up with a plan. First would be x-rays, an ultrasound, and blood work to see if the cancer had spread anywhere else yet. The tests were to be done at Stillwater. Results were sent to New York and the University of Minnesota where, in short order, Ruby would visit oncologist Dr. Henson.

I called Rob Olson who also had been following Ruby's life over at Fox News. He reacted instantly with an excellent story that day. Newspapers likewise soon followed with their own pieces. One of the reporters had not long ago returned from Iraq and Afghanistan as an imbedded reporter for *Stars and Stripes*. A deeply interesting fellow, he was a dog lover and shared his perspective from those hot zones and how poorly the locals treat their dogs. The local NBC television station did a terrific story as well, spending a number of hours at the University of Minnesota veterinarian hospital with Ruby and her oncologist. The media often asked about Ruby's Milk-Bone box while doing these update stories. I had no answers. It was getting very embarrassing.

The results of the tests were hopeful and brightened my outlook. There was no "mother tumor," no sign it had spread anywhere. It was determined that the cancer had been very slow growing up to that point. Options were presented: chemotherapy—great for fast spreading or "hot" cancer, not so good on slow-growing cancer, plus I'd heard so much about side effects. Radiation—pin-point accuracy, would kill cancer in the leg if any remained, but the problem was that it was a twenty-three-day protocol and Ruby would be put under every day, and it too had possible unpleasant side effects. Surgery—get very aggressive about removing additional tissue. Oncologists seem to feel there are never wide enough margins taken during surgery. I was asked to think things over and get back to them.

By this time, it was early November. I was frozen with indecision. The thought of any of the three alternatives filled me with dread. But the clock was ticking. In the middle of everything I contacted Milk-Bone, asking hard questions about the boxes. No response.

Meanwhile, a complication arrived in the form of an offer from the City of Stillwater convention and tourism bureau. They wanted to hire Ruby and myself as Santa and his helper from late November through December 23. It was good money, and we would work seven days a week. What a coup for Ruby! Imagine a city that actually invited a pit bull to meet and greet the public and attend various functions with scores of children present. Upscale, historic 1880s Stillwater on the St. Croix River is a city just barely east of St.

Paul/Minneapolis. What a wonderful opportunity for Ruby, for the breed, for rescue dogs. And we sure could use the money. The offer was so very tempting, but the timing was so very bad.

I called Dr. Henson at the university. Explaining the situation, I asked if because the cancer was slow growing, we could wait until after the holidays for treatment or surgery. What was the danger? What option would he choose? He said the greatest danger of having it spread would have been right after the first surgery. He felt we could wait until after Christmas, but not much longer. He also said, "You know, Pat, she may be cured now. There's no sign of it spreading, but I am uncomfortable with the narrow margins from the first surgery. If Ruby were my dog, I'd go in again and clean it out well. Perhaps followed by radiation."

So the decision was made. We would take the job, and come January Ruby would go in for surgery. But was it the right move? Much soul searching and second guessing continued daily. For now, thinking about the holiday season was far more pleasant than thinking about cancer.

No doubt about it, we had a blast! A terrific PR shot of Ruby and me dressed in our festive best was taken by In Studio, a local photography shop. In it, I am appropriately jolly, but Ruby, wearing an elfin hat complete with correct ears was irresistible! It was a hit, seen everywhere, including in a half-page spread in the St. Paul paper along with a Ruby update. We were caught off guard by the number of people who wanted to buy autographed copies of the picture.

During the month of December, it was part of our job description to waltz up and down the main street, greeting shoppers, stopping by stores and restaurants, and attending special events. Ruby and I met people from England, Australia, Sweden, and Germany as well as the regulars. So many holiday shoppers wanted to have their picture taken with Santa and his helper, Santapaws, that Ruby and I

141

felt like rock stars! I had played Santa Claus many times before, but always in senior residences or nursing homes. This was wild! Some folks wanted us with family members in their Christmas cards. Others wanted just Granny sitting on Santa's lap. One portly middle-aged couple sporting Santa hats wanted a picture snapped with one on each knee…ugh! The list goes on and on with fun, goofy, straight, and one risqué request that made Santa's cheeks even rosier than usual. That request was turned down, but hey at my age, it was a compliment. Everyone who took a picture insisted that Ruby be included as well. Old Santa's lap and knees had quite a workout that month.

But it was the kids who were the most fun, and a direct link to some of my happier childhood memories. There were the sweet and tender children in awe of Santa, barely loud enough to tell me what they wanted. Some even forgot what to ask for. Others were very outgoing and frank about their desires, complete with written lists and second choices. Santa's elves would have to work overtime to fill their orders. Looking up into the parents' pleading eyes, saying "please don't promise everything," we'd do our best to tone things down. Some kids were skeptical, perhaps doing this to humor their parents who just wanted to see one more season of childhood innocence. These kids may have been skeptical, but they still hedged their bets. Last, tossed into the mix, were children who wanted nothing to do with this large man in a very red suit. No matter what bargaining chip Mom and Dad used, it went for naught as the kids screamed, cried, and occasionally spit up. Eventually, they could be coaxed to get close enough to pet Ruby, who was apparently less intimidating than I was. That was the common thread among the kids. They loved her, and she had kisses for all of them. Ruby was not a slobbery kisser, just quick little tags. They were curious about her of course, but it was some of the more savvy and vocal children who just had to ask, "What's a dog got to do with Santa Claus?"

My answer was ready. "She's my crew chief. She barks out orders to the reindeer! Oh! Oh! Oh!" Oddly, to the kids it made sense. To the adults, it was an appreciated pun topped with a chuckle. Ruby enjoyed herself immensely. But an unexpected side effect of all this hands-on socializing had her back in service dog training for a refresher course. With all of the attention, petting, close interaction, and praise, she began to self-start in dealing with the public. That is, going to people on her own if someone called to her or looked particularly interesting. As a service dog, it was not allowed. It didn't take long though, and she was back in the fold. As much fun as our new roles were, come January reality looked us square in the eye. Ruby must go under the knife. But first Milk-Bone stirred things up, yet again.

In mid-December, I received an email from the IC Group representing Milk-Bone. The boxes would now not be out until May, almost a year and a half after the 100-year anniversary "Make a Milk-Bone Moment" contest had ended. Also, there was a change. Wyatt and Ruby would no longer have their own boxes. Their pictures would now be together on the back of a box. I thought, "Gee, this will be fun when I have to tell the media who must be wondering about me with all of the excuses I've been giving them." I forwarded a copy of the email from IC Group to all of Ruby's media friends just to let them know we weren't blowing smoke. I was sick and tired of it all. As is the case when cancer strikes a family, Ruby's illness had put things in a proper perspective.

Let us put this whole caper to bed. I had never intended to cast any doubt on Milk-Bone's products. We continued to give our dogs Milk-Bone biscuits. We saluted its programs to help supply service dogs to those in need and K-9s for various police departments—worthy causes both.

After all we went through with Milk-Bone, it may be difficult for the reader to understand, but I was, from the bottom of my heart, deeply grateful to the company for giving us memories that would be with me until my last breath. Ruby and I shared some wonderful experiences in our association with them that we otherwise would never have had. We met some terrific people along the way, including Jason Wehner, senior brand manager. It also helped open some doors. Thing is, it didn't have to end this way. But this is corporate America. Things can and do happen. Sometimes the right hand doesn't know what the left hand is up to. From my point of view, Milk-Bone was a good, well-run, very profitable company. It just seemed that not everyone there was aware of some questionable decisions made, and how things were handled, at least in regard to the contest. But I do wish them well.

Now had come the time I had so feared: Ruby's surgery. What would they find? Was my decision to delay going to cost her dearly? I had wanted one more adventure with Ruby in case the operation didn't go well. Now I was regretting my selfishness.

Early morning on a Thursday, I brought her to the university. Dr. Diana Allevato would perform the surgery. She had seen Ruby twice before, calling her beautiful and wonderfully behaved. I waited around a couple of hours, but knew I wouldn't be seeing Ruby until later. I left to wait for the call.

Early afternoon, the doctor was on the phone. "Everything went well. But Pat, I was very aggressive in removing additional tissue. Be prepared for a very long incision. We'll have the results of the tests next week, and she can go home later today."

I didn't care about the long incision or a scar. Neither would Ruby. I just wanted her back home safe, happy, and healthy. But it was going to be a long week until the results came back.

Ruby's homecoming was anticlimactic. Even though she looked like Frankenpup with that seven-inch incision running from about her hip down past her knee, Ruby acted as if she never had surgery. She wanted to run about the house, play with the other dogs, and jump up on our laps. We put a stop to that! In fact, Ruby was more active right after the operation than normal.

We were told the pain pills sent home for her comfort would make her sleepy. Ha! Ruby also earned herself an E-collar as a result of licking, cleaning, and nibbling on her leg. She was not happy about this. Standing stiff legged in front of me when first installed, the poor thing gave me those eyes every dog owner knows well. "Dad, ohhh the indignity of wearing this, this thing! What have I done to deserve this? Please remove it!"

Within a couple of days, though, the little diva was motoring around the house quite nicely. The E-collar was made of a clear material which helped, I'm sure. To Ruby's credit, she never panicked but set about learning to live with it to an amazing degree. She never even tried to remove it.

A week had passed since Ruby's date with the doctor. The expected call came almost on cue. Dr. Allevato's voice, bright and strong, announced the wide margins were clean and clear of any cancer. Nothing was left, nothing had spread! Oncologist Dr. Henson said radiation was still an option, but also felt that given the amount of tissue removed and the test results, it just may be overkill. Ruby had been given a second chance at life. My emotions ran strong and unimpeded. Such true happiness a person feels only too seldom in life. Heck, I'd been given a second chance, too.

As Ruby continued to heal, I took time to reflect on her life and how it had changed mine. Who could have imagined a little unwanted dog left to die would have come so far and touched so many lives in such a positive way, especially mine? Then I thought about all of the lonely, unwanted dogs out there no matter what the breed. Through all the abandonment, abuse, and neglect, the great majority of them came out of it with an incredible resilience, boundless love, and devotion when given a forever home.

EPILOGUE

If you have it in your heart, if you have the time, volunteer at a local shelter or rescue facility. Better yet, consider fostering. Best of all, consider adoption. But please don't take the responsibilities lightly. Take stock of every aspect of the decision you make. The lives of wonderful, living little beings are on the line. They will trust you all their live long days. As it is said, "May you be the person your dog thinks you are." Sometimes it takes patience when dealing with possible past issues. It may take hard work. It should always include some degree of training. Every minute you spend with your new family member nurturing, loving, and training them will indeed pay off in huge dividends. While I certainly recommend Cesar Millan's books as a great guide to help you along, there are other excellent training books available as well. But whenever possible, formal dog training classes are a must.

You never know where your rescue dog may take you. Maybe your new friend won't end up like Ruby. Maybe they'll do her one better. But they don't have to. The possibilities for family fun, fulfillment, and community enrichment are endless. Obedience classes, agility and fly ball competition, volunteer search and rescue are just a sampling of the rewarding things you can do with Fido. Let's not forget about pet therapy. There is a great need in a wide variety of venues...hospitals, senior residences, children's hospitals, and schools. You cannot possibly know all the lives you will touch and in what way your visits make a difference. Sometimes, stories of your time well spent come back to you months or even years later. It is a big win all the way around, for the dog, you, your family, and the lives of hurting, lonely, ill, or handicapped individuals who want to feel gentle, warm love. You'll feel good knowing you've made a difference.

These days, recovered, Ruby is as busy as ever. She was invited by the Miami Coalition against breed-specific legislation to help premier a two-hour documentary on breed-specific legislation called *Beyond the Myth*. While there, Ruby spent some time with patients at Hialeah Hospital and a rehab center. Her visit was a resounding success as the staff warmly welcomed Ruby with opened hearts. With two people from the *Miami Herald,* hospital administrators, a bevy of doctors, PR people, nurses, therapists, a photographer, plus a couple of curious onlookers all following Ruby from room to room, she felt like a movie star...acted like one, too. She always seemed to turn a bit so the cameras would get her "good side." Pit bulls aren't allowed in Miami, but because of her status as a service dog certified to ADI standards and the federal laws regarding service dogs, Ruby was there with bells on. The Miami trip wasn't all work. The diva spent a little time at the beach and Ocean Drive looking cool and gathering attention. Ruby even waltzed by a startled cop! We'll never forget the good people of the Miami Coalition who took such good care of Ruby and me...perhaps too good. Okay, I'll admit it, we were spoiled rotten. Then dear Lynn had to deal with us when we returned. Poor thing!

Back home, Ruby was considering another play and scheduling more personal appearances to other states for rescue group fundraisers as a celebrity dog. There, she will be donating a portion of her book sales to help the effort. Trips are in the works to Chicago again as well as New York. And yes, Ruby still visits her senior citizens.

Let's not forget about the pack she has to run. Like Katie from a few years ago, Ruby rules with a velvet paw. If horseplay gets a little too rough, she'll bump or nose them apart. A great example of her position occurred just the other night. Ruby was late coming to bed. I was quietly listening to an old radio program, and Lynn was comfortably asleep. Molly had stealthily hopped up on the bed in Ruby's empty position. Soon she was gently sawing wood. A few minutes later, I heard Ruby come up the stairs and stop at the doorway. She said nothing, not a growl, not a whine, not a whimper—absolutely silent. Molly stirred from her sleep, jumped down, and curled up on a nearby dog bed. Ruby sailed up to her rightful position on our bed. Now that's power!

You'd be right to ask, "Does Ruby ever get time to be just a dog to run free and rip it up in that one-acre, fenced-in backyard, to go for long walks in the country, to smell the mysterious scents floating on the wind, to take a lazy snooze in the sun, to pick up the trail of a rabbit recently passed by?" It is a world that is exclusively hers. A world I can never fully know. I am perhaps guilty of not permitting her to re-enter that world as often as I should. But in my recent solemn promise to Ruby, that will change and we'll both be better for it.

It has been wonderful sharing the incredible, exciting, sometimes wild odyssey that has been Ruby's life. I thank her from the deepest recesses of my very soul. She has selflessly given me more than I could ever return.

Our adventures are far from over. On some quiet day when we least expect it, in will come a phone call or an email. Or perhaps one morning, coffee cup in one hand, sheet of paper in the other, Lynn will come into the den. "Hon, here's something Ruby and you should consider..."

ABOUT THE AUTHOR

Patrick Bettendorf lives with his wife, Lynn; youngest daughter, Sadie; and "the tribe" in a small country town just northeast of St. Paul/Minneapolis. He has been a male model, an actor of stage and industrial training films, a radio personality, and a scriptwriter.

He is founder and managing director of Duck Soup Players theater company. Since 1969, Duck Soup Players has brought comedy productions to those who can't easily get out such as those living in senior residences or hospitals, to enjoy all that the community has to offer. The players also did seven USO tours of VA hospitals and remote military bases to rave reviews. In 1983, Duck Soup Players was invited by President Reagan to Washington, DC, to help celebrate the USO's fortieth anniversary. It was during his time with the players that Patrick saw the painful yearning the residents and patients had for a sense of normalcy in their lives, and a need for something from happier times, primarily pets. Being a dog lover, he set a path to do something about it. In the helping of others, he has healed himself.

CANINE BLOOD DONATIONS

Wyatt and I had a wonderful time meeting Pat and Ruby in Los Angeles and Chicago. I would like to thank them for giving us a chance to educate the readers about canine blood donations.

As an emergency veterinarian, I understand the importance of having a blood supply available for emergencies. We could not have saved many of the lives at our clinic without this important biological. Most of us do not think about this until a crisis hits in our fur children. In my experience, people are so grateful for this lifesaving option for their pet and are eager to learn more and "pay it forward." It is my and Wyatt's mission to inspire you to learn more about this life-saving donation.

Before letting you know how you can help with this shortage, let me share with you a few facts about canine blood.

Dogs do have a number of different blood types. But generally two main types are categorized: 1.1 negative ("universal" donor) and 1.1 positive. In an emergency, we typically use "universal" blood since there is usually no time to blood type the recipient. Blood types are not breed specific, so a Great Dane could donate to a Chihuahua. There are certain breeds, however, that tend to be universal blood types, such as greyhounds, boxers, Dobermans, pit bulls, and German Shepherds. Mixed breeds can be universal donors as well. 1.1 positive is the most common blood type. Breeds that tend to be 1.1 positive are golden retrievers and Labrador retrievers.

Typically during a donation, one pint of blood is drawn. This pint can be used to save up to four lives. The blood is usually separated into its components: packed red blood cells and plasma. Transfusions of catastrophic proportion may use whole blood, but typically only components are needed. Just a few of the uses for packed red blood cells are trauma, abdominal hemorrhage, certain cancers, and immune-mediated diseases. Plasma is used for certain rat poisons, severe inflammatory processes, and DIC.

The requirements and incentives for canine donors vary by facility. Generally, dogs need to be between 1–8 years of age, in good health, over 50 pounds, current on vaccinations and heartworm prevention, unmedicated, and have a friendly and even-tempered disposition.

Many blood banks, including the Eastern Veterinary Blood Bank, where Wyatt donates, are volunteer blood banks. This means that the dogs are brought in by owners once every seven weeks to donate blood. The actual process only takes about five minutes and the donors can eat treats through the entire donation. Typically they lie on the table and get plenty of love and attention.

Many veterinary schools and larger clinics also use volunteer donors. Many programs offer some type of free medical care for your dog and screen your dog yearly for certain tick-borne and metabolic diseases to make sure your dog and his/her blood are healthy.

Some larger blood banks house the dogs they use for blood collection. The dogs are usually retired racing greyhounds and dogs from shelters, who were slated for euthanasia. These blood banks use the dogs as blood donors and then adopt them into their forever homes. For more information and answers to questions, please visit my website at www.DrJacquelineandWyatt.com.

Please consider letting your dog become a canine hero like Wyatt by donating blood.